CSS

Beginners Guide to CSS to Master Your Web Designing

JOSH STEVEN

TABLE OF CONTENTS

Introduction 1

Chapter 1: What is CSS? 3

Chapter 2: CSS Selectors and Insertion 13

Chapter 3: CSS Margins, Padding, and Width 31

Chapter 4: CSS Borders, Background, etc… 57

Chapter 6: CSS Colors 83

Chapter 7: CSS Outline, Boxes 99

Chapter 8: CSS Links, Tables, and Forms 107

Chapter 9: CSS Images and Lists 128

Chapter 10: CSS Rounded Corners 144

Chapter 11: CSS Layout, Float and Inline-Block 155

Chapter 12: Navigation Bar 169

Conclusion 202

References 204

Introduction

Cascading Style Sheets or CSS is the hot-on-demand language for designing of a website. Internet browsers efficiently read it and also support it well. This language is quite easy to learn and also offers an easier way to apply different types of styles on the HTML element. If you try to apply the same in HTML, you will have to go through an excruciating code that would be difficult to write and hard to understand.

On the other hand, CSS can help you modularize the website. Modular code offers programmers an elevated amount of efficiency and consistency in the design and a way easier maintenance. This is the new standard in the web designing industry, and this is going to stay for many years to come.

CSS is much easier to update and modify. It offers excellent formatting options and has a very lightweight code. CSS pages are very light, and they are easier to download compared to some other pages that are created in some other programming language. It also helps you in search engine optimization (SEO).

Coming back to a faster web page download time, CSS involves a lot less coding than many other languages. This means that when you style a table, you will have to write a short amount of code in

CSS compared to many of the other computer languages. Usually, when a browser sees a table on your web page, it has to read the code twice, once to understand how you have structured the table, and a second time to display the content that is inside the table. This double reading of web pages slows down the downloading time which affects the quality of your website. This may result in a decrease in website traffic as your visitors will find it frustrating to wait for the page to download. The end result can be a loss of customers and ultimately a loss of money.

Similarly, images also are the heaviest features on a website, and they take time to download. They tend to slow down your web pages considerably. The fact is that you can optimize them and make them smaller, but still, they will be larger than written lines of code. As a result, the browser may dispatch another request to the server. As your CSS is inside a single file, the browser will put the cache the code, and it won't be needing to download it again for the remaining pages of the website.

CSS offers more control over the presentation of the web pages. You can adjust the font size, the font style, the font type, and the font color. You can also add spacing around the text by the padding feature. You can add images in the text in different shapes. Also, you will be able to choose from a wide range of colors to make your tables, lists, and paragraphs meaningful. You can take up a single color and make it dark or light. CSS offers great flexibility in terms of creating and adjusting the code. For example, if you have lots of images on your page, you can put them in the last after some text, so that your visitors will have something to remain busy until the images are fully downloaded on the web page.

Chapter 1

What is CSS?

This chapter will explain how you can make your web pages exceptionally good looking with the help of CSS. You will learn how CSS gives you the best control over the design of your website. CSS empowers developers to create their own rules for designing websites. It gives them the freedom to decide how a specific element should appear on the web page. If the background is white, you can choose to display the elements on the page in blue or gray so that they appear well when someone visits your website. You can add different colors to the headings and make a particular piece of text italic or bold as you think suits best.

When you have learned the key to write a CSS rule, you will be able to maneuver several CSS properties that you can use while designing a web page. This chapter will walk you through the way CSS works, teach you how you can write CSS rules, and then show you how you can integrate CSS into HTML pages.

If you want to understand CSS, you should think of every HTML as having a box around it that is invisible. Let's first create a simple HTML page and display it in the browser. This is what I see in the HTML page sample.

I will tell you a story about an eagle.

Once, there was an eagle that flew higher in the skies,

Touching upon the tip of the mountains.

One day she found a ring stuck in the branch of an apple tree.

She took it and flew to her nest. While playing with it, she got her head stuck in it.

She didn't panic or hit her head on the stump of a tree to get rid of it.

Instead, she embraced it as a mark of distinction among fellow eagles.

Then, one day she drenched her head in oil and the ring came off of her neck.

On the top, you can see the heading 1. After that, the body of the page shows you the entire story. Let's start and add some design to our page.

```
<html>
<head>
<style>
body {
    background-color: pink;
}
h1 {
```

```
    color: gray;
    text-align: left;
}
p {
    font-family: georgia;
    font-size: 25px;
}
</style>
</head>
<body>
<h1>I will tell you a story about an eagle.</h1>
<p> Once, there was an eagle that flew higher in
the skies,
<br> touching upon the tip of the mountains.
<br> One day she found a ring stuck in the
branch of an apple tree.
<br> She took it and flew to her nest. While
playing with it, she got her head stuck in it.
<br> She didn't panic or hit her head on the
stump of a tree to get rid of it.
<br> Instead, she embraced it as a mark of
distinction among fellow eagles.
<br> Then, one day she drenched her head in oil
and the ring came off of her neck.</p>
</body>
</html>
```

Now that you have seen how you can add designs to a web page. Let's analyze CSS syntax. CSS syntax consists of a selector along with a declaration block. Let's analyze the following code snippet.

```
h1 {
    color: gray;
    text-align: left;
}
```

In the above code, h1 is called a selector. Color is called property. Pink is known as value. The font-size is known as property, while 25px is called value. The phrase color: pink is known as a declaration.

The selectors point to the HTML element that you need to style. In the declaration block, you can find one or more declarations that are separated by semicolons. In each declaration, you can find a CSS property and its value, as seen in the above example. Don't forget to include a semicolon in the end. Also, always take care that curly braces fully encircle declaration blocks. I will change the values of declaration blocks. Let's see how to do that.

```
<html>
<head>
<style>
body {
    background-color: gray;
}
h1 {
    color: black;
```

```
    text-align: center;
  }
  p {
    font-family: ariel;
    font-size: 20px;
  }
  </style>
  </head>
  <body>
  <h1> I will tell you a story about an
  eagle.</h1>
  <p> Once, there was an eagle that flew higher in
  the skies,
  <br> touching upon the tip of the mountains.
  <br> One day she found a ring stuck in the
  branch of an apple tree.
  <br> She took it and flew to her nest. While
  playing with it, she got her head stuck in it.
  <br> She didn't panic or hit her head on the
  stump of a tree to get rid of it.
  <br> Instead, she embraced it as a mark of
  distinction among fellow eagles.
  <br> Then, one day she drenched her head in oil
  and the ring came off of her neck.</p>
  </body>
  </html>
```

Save the file with .html extension and then open it in a browser. You can see that the background color, font size and style have changed.

Let's change the code one more time to clear the concepts in our minds.

```html
<html>
<head>
<style>
body {
   background-color: azure;
}
h1 {
   color: blue;
   text-align: center;
}
p {
   font-family: times new roman;
   font-size: 22px;
}
</style>
</head>
<body>
<h1>I will tell you a story about an eagle.</h1>
<p> Once, there was an eagle that flew higher in the skies,
<br> touching upon the tip of the mountains.
<br> One day she found a ring stuck in the branch of an apple tree.
<br> She took it and flew to her nest. While playing with it, she got her head stuck in it.
```

```
<br> She didn't panic or hit her head on the
stump of a tree to get rid of it.
<br> Instead, she embraced it as a mark of
distinction among fellow eagles.
<br> Then, one day she drenched her head in oil
and the ring came off of her neck.</p></body>
</html>
```

The background will be azure, and font size and style will be changed. You can practice this code in your Note ++ editor.

Adding a Comment

You can add comments in your code to use as a reference later on for remembering what you have been doing. You can use a slash and * for adding a comment in the code. I have added three comments at different points in the code. Let's see how they look. I will be using the same code example for adding comments.

```
<html>
<head>
<style>
/* Now, we will add style to the body, heading,
and paragraph.
body {
    background-color: azure;
}
/* You can see CSS property and declaration
h1 {
    color: blue;
```

9

```
    text-align: center;
}
/* We are styling CSS paragraphs below
p {
    font-family: times new roman;
    font-size: 22px;
}
</style>
</head>
<body>
<h1>I will tell you a story about an eagle.</h1>
<p> Once, there was an eagle that flew higher in
the skies,
<br> touching upon the tip of the mountains.
<br> One day she found a ring stuck in the
branch of an apple tree.
<br> She took it and flew to her nest. While
playing with it, she got her head stuck in it.
<br> She didn't panic or hit her head on the
stump of a tree to get rid of it.
<br> Instead, she embraced it as a mark of
distinction among fellow eagles.
<br> Then, one day she drenched her head in oil
and the ring came off of her neck.</p>
.</p>
</body>
</html>
```

Comments won't be displayed on the page. The most common mistake you can make while adding comments to the code is leaving them open at the end. If you commit this kind of mistake, your code will stop working. There will no design on your page. Let's see the error.

```html
<html>
<head>
<style>
/* Now, we will add style to the body, heading, and paragraph.
body {
  background-color: azure;
}
/* You can see CSS property and declaration
h1 {
  color: blue;
  text-align: center;
}
/* We are styling CSS paragraphs below
p {
  font-family: times new roman;
  font-size: 22px;
}
</style>
</head>
<body>
<h1>I will tell you a story about an eagle.</h1>
```

```
<p> Once, there was an eagle that flew higher in
the skies,

<br> touching upon the tip of the mountains.

<br> One day she found a ring stuck in the
branch of an apple tree.

<br> She took it and flew to her nest. While
playing with it, she got her head stuck in it.

<br> She didn't panic or hit her head on the
stump of a tree to get rid of it.

<br> Instead, she embraced it as a mark of
distinction among fellow eagles.

<br> Then, one day she drenched her head in oil
and the ring came off of her neck.</p>

</body>

</html>
```

(CSS Syntax, n.d)

Chapter 2

CSS Selectors and Insertion

CSS selectors are typically used to locate the HTML elements that you need to add style to. Different types of CSS selectors would allow you to target different HTML elements. One thing to note is that CSS selectors usually are case sensitive. Therefore, you should be careful while matching elements and names. Some selectors are pretty advanced that would allow you to partially or entirely select HTML elements.

```css
h1 {
   color: blue;
   text-align: center;
}
/* We are styling CSS paragraphs below
p {
   font-family: times new roman;
   font-size: 22px;
}
```

In the above example, we can see that two HTML elements have been selected, to which I have added the required values.

CSS id Selector

CSS id selector is also a very interesting feature of this language. If you want to style a certain part of the paragraph, the id selector is the way to go. This special selector makes use of a special id attribute of the HTML element to select the element that you want to style. Each id is unique or each element on the same page. If you keep it the same for different elements, the editor will be unable to recognize it. So does the browser. When you have created an id selector, you can use it for styling by inserting a hash (#) before the id of that specific element.

```
<html>
<head>
<style>
body {
    background-color: white;
}
h1 {
    color: blue;
    text-align: center;
}
#para1 {
    text-align: left;
    color: red;
}
p {
    font-family: times new roman;
```

```
    font-size: 22px;
}
</style>
</head>
<body>
<h1>I will tell you a story about an eagle.</h1>
<p id="para1"> Once, there was an eagle that
flew higher in the skies,
<br> touching upon the tip of the mountains </p>
<p> One day she found a ring stuck in the branch
of an apple tree.
<br> She took it and flew to her nest. While
playing with it, she got her head stuck in it.
<br> She didn't panic or hit her head on the
stump of a tree to get rid of it.
<br> Instead, she embraced it as a mark of
distinction among fellow eagles.
<br> Then, one day she drenched her head in oil
and the ring came off of her neck.</p>
</body>
</html>
```

Here is the result in the web browser.

I will tell you a story about an eagle.

Once, there was an eagle that flew higher in the skies, touching upon the tip of the mountains

One day she found a ring stuck in the branch of an apple tree. She took it and flew to her nest. While playing with it, she got her head stuck in it.

She didn't panic or hit her head on the stump of a tree to get rid of it.

Instead, she embraced it as a mark of distinction among fellow eagles.

Then, one day she drenched her head in oil and the ring came off of her neck.

CSS Class Selector

This type of selector selects HTML elements that have a particular class attribute. You have to use a period (.) to select HTML elements. You will have to add the class name after the period. Let's try to understand how the class selector works by creating an example. I will select another HTML element with the help of the class selector. Let's see how to do that.

```
<html>
<head>
<style>
.center {
    text-align: left;
    color: orange;
}
body {
```

```
  background-color: white;
}
h1 {
  color: blue;
  text-align: center;
}
p {
  font-family: times new roman;
  font-size: 22px;
}
</style>
</head>
<body>
<h1 class="center">I will tell you a story about an eagle.</h1>
<p> Once, there was an eagle that flew higher in the skies,
<br> touching upon the tip of the mountains </p>
<p> One day she found a ring stuck in the branch of an apple tree.
<br> She took it and flew to her nest. While playing with it, she got her head stuck in it.
<br> She didn't panic or hit her head on the stump of a tree to get rid of it.
<br> Instead, she embraced it as a mark of distinction among fellow eagles.
<br> Then, one day she drenched her head in oil and the ring came off of her neck.</p>
.</p>
```

```
</body>
</html>
```

You can try the above code in the editor and check out the results. Let's try to apply the class selector on another HTML element.

```
<html>
<head>
<style>
.center {
    text-align: left;
    color: orange;
}
body {
    background-color: white;
}
h1 {
    color: blue;
    text-align: center;
}
p {
    font-family: times new roman;
    font-size: 22px;
}
</style>
</head>
```

```
<body>

<h1>I will tell you a story about an eagle.</h1>

<p class="center"> Once, there was an eagle that
flew higher in the skies,

<br> touching upon the tip of the mountains </p>

<p> One day she found a ring stuck in the branch
of an apple tree.

<br> She took it and flew to her nest. While
playing with it, she got her head into it.

<br> She didn't panic and hit her head in the
stump of the tree to get rid of it.

<br> Instead, she embraced it as a mark of
distinction among fellow eagles.

<br> Then one day she drenched her head in oil
and the ring moved out of her neck.</p>

</body>

</html>
```

If you try it out yourself, you will be able to see that the class selector has successfully changed the style of the entire paragraph. When you have published this page, you can change the code and see how it affects the results. CSS classes allow us to make changes in the code in a fast manner. We can apply the change on an entire page of code in a blink of an eye.

CSS Universal Selector

This is not specific to a single HTML element but will affect each of them. We are going to indicate the CSS universal selector with the (*) symbol. This feature greatly helps when you have to apply a specific design to a complete page. Let's see how it happens.

```
<html>
<head>
<style>
* {
    text-align: left;
    color: orange;
}
</style>
</head>
<body>
<h1>I will tell you a story about an eagle.</h1>
<p class="center"> Once, there was an eagle that
flew high in the skies,<br> touching upon the
tip of the mountains.</p>
<p> One day she found a ring, stuck in the
branch of an apple tree.
<br> She took it and flew to her nest. While
playing with it, she got her head stuck into it.
<br> She didn't panic and hit her head into the
stump of the tree to get rid of it.
<br> Instead, she embraced it as a mark of
distinction among fellow eagles.
<br> Then one day she drenched her head in oil
and the ring moved out of her neck.</p>
</body>
</html>
```

CSS Grouping Selector

This grouping selector selects all HTML elements that contain the same style definitions. Let's take a look at the CSS code given as under.

```
<html>
<head>
<style>
h1, p {
    text-align: left;
    color: green;
}
</style>
</head>
<body>
<h1>I will tell you a story about an eagle.</h1>
<p> Once, there was an eagle that flew high in
the skies,
<br> touching upon the tip of the mountains.
<br> One day she found a ring, stuck in the
branch of an apple tree.
<br> She took it and flew to her nest. While
playing with it, she got her head stuck into it.
<br> She didn't panic and hit her head into the
stump of the tree to get rid of it.
<br> Instead, she embraced it as a mark of
distinction among fellow eagles.
<br> Then one day she drenched her head in oil
and the ring moved out of her neck.</p>
```

```
</body>
</html>
```

In the next code snippet, I will be adding an h2 heading in the page and see how the group selector works.

```
<html>
<head>
<style>
head, h1, p {
    text-align: left;
    color: green;
}
</style>
</head>
<body>
<h1>I will tell you a story about an eagle.</h1>
<h2>This is a short story.</h2>
<p> Once, there was an eagle that flew high in
the skies,
<br> touching upon the tip of the mountains.
<br> One day she found a ring, stuck in the
branch of an apple tree.
<br> She took it and flew to her nest. While
playing with it, she got her head stuck into it.
<br> She didn't panic and hit her head into the
stump of the tree to get rid of it.
<br> Instead, she embraced it as a mark of
distinction among fellow eagles.
```

```
<br> Then one day she drenched her head in oil
and the ring moved out of her neck.</p>
</body>
</html>
```

Let's see the results.

I will tell you a story about an eagle.

This is a short story.

Once, there was an eagle that flew high in the skies,
touching upon the tip of the mountains.
One day she found a ring stuck in the branch of an apple tree.
She took it and flew to her nest. While playing with it, she got her
head stuck into it.
She didn't panic and hit her head into the stump of the tree to get rid
of it.
Instead, she embraced it as a mark of distinction among fellow
eagles.
Then one day, she drenched her head in oil, and the ring moved out
of her neck.

(CSS Selectors, n.d)

CSS works by linking rules to HTML elements on your page. These
rules decide how certain elements are displayed, as you have seen in
different examples. We have learned in detail how to apply selectors
on HTML elements on a web page.

How to Insert CSS into HTML Elements

You can use <link> element in the HTML document that we have been using to instruct the browser where it can find the CSS file that you have to use to design your web page. The <link> element is an empty element as there is no need for a closing tag. There are generally three attributes for this element.

1. href
   This tells the path that leads to the CSS file. You can put a CSS file in a folder that you can name as styles or css.

2. type
   The second attribute tells the browser about the type of the document.

3. rel
   This one tells the browser about the relationship between an HTML page as well as the css file it is linked to.

Now let's take a look at different types of inserting CSS into an HTML document.

External CSS

You can create a CSS file and then add it to an HTML document externally. This is how you will be able to change the design of your website by switching to a different file with a single click. You have to include a reference to an external style sheet on each HTML page. You will have to insert the <link> in the head section. Let's see how it happens.

```html
<html>

<head>

<link rel="stylesheet" type="text/css"
href="mystylecss.css">

</head>

<body>

<h1>I will tell you a story about an eagle.</h1>

<h2>This is a short story.</h2>

<p> Once, there was an eagle that flew high in
the skies,

<br> touching upon the tip of the mountains.

<br> One day she found a ring, stuck in the
branch of an apple tree.

<br> She took it and flew to her nest. While
playing with it, she got her head stuck into it.

<br> She didn't panic and hit her head into the
stump of the tree to get rid of it.

<br> Instead, she embraced it as a mark of
distinction among fellow eagles.

<br> Then one day she drenched her head in oil
and the ring moved out of her neck.</p>

</body>

</html>
```

The above is the HTML document that we have to use to link to our CSS stylesheet. Now let's create an external CSS stylesheet. If you are using Notepad ++, you can create a new file in the same editor besides the HTML document and create the CSS file. When you are done with the sheet, and you get ready to save it, you should add .css extension to the end of the name of the file. Let's create the CSS stylesheet.

```
body {
   background-color: pink;
}
h1 {
   color: blue;
   margin-left: 25px;
}
```

Internal CSS

The external way of linking HTML document to CSS style sheet is more viable for large CSS designs which tend to confuse you if you include them in HTML document. What if the HTML document is a short one? To solve this problem, you can use the internal style sheet that is quite suitable for a shorter HTML page. Also, you will have to add the <style> tag to the document. Let's see how to do that.

```
<html>
<head>
<style>
body {
   background-color: orange;
}
h1 {
   color: blue;
   margin-left: 25px;
```

```
    }
</style>
</head>
<body>
<h1>I will tell you a story about an eagle.</h1>
<h2>This is a short story.</h2>
<p> Once, there was an eagle that flew high in
the skies,
<br> touching upon the tip of the mountains.
<br> One day she found a ring, stuck in the
branch of an apple tree.
<br> She took it and flew to her nest. While
playing with it, she got her head stuck into it.
<br> She didn't panic and hit her head into the
stump of the tree to get rid of it.
<br> Instead, she embraced it as a mark of
distinction among fellow eagles.
<br> Then one day she drenched her head in oil
and the ring moved out of her neck.</p>
</body>
</html>
```

If you are building a single-page website, internal CSS is a good option, but in case you are building a multipage website, you are going to need an external CSS style sheet to keep things simple. That's how you can apply the same color scheme to different pages instead of repeating them on each page. You will be able to keep the content separate, so it will be easier to read the HTML code. When you have to change the styles in the webpage, you can do that by changing a single line in the code.

Inline CSS

There is a third option for simple style changes. You can use inline CSS to apply style on single HTML elements. I will be adding inline styles to different elements on a CSS page. You can add any CSS property in the style attribute.

```
<html>

<body>

<h1>I will tell you a story about an eagle.</h1>

<h2 style="color:gray;margin-left:25px;">This is a short story.</h2>

<p> Once, there was an eagle that flew high in the skies,

<br> touching upon the tip of the mountains.

<br> One day she found a ring, stuck in the branch of an apple tree.

<br> She took it and flew to her nest. While playing with it, she got her head stuck into it.

<br> She didn't panic and hit her head into the stump of the tree to get rid of it.

<br> Instead, she embraced it as a mark of distinction among fellow eagles.

<br> Then one day she drenched her head in oil and the ring moved out of her neck.</p>

</body>

</html>
```

The result should be displayed as under:

I will tell you a story about an eagle.

This is a short story.

Once, there was an eagle that flew high in the skies, touching upon the tip of the mountains.
One day she found a ring stuck in the branch of an apple tree.
She took it and flew to her nest. While playing with it, she got her head stuck into it.
She didn't panic and hit her head into the stump of the tree to get rid of it.
Instead, she embraced it as a mark of distinction among fellow eagles.
Then one day, she drenched her head in oil, and the ring moved out of her neck.

Now in the following code snippet, I will add the inline style to the paragraph. In this way, you can be able to add styles to individual HTML elements such as headings and paragraphs. This is important because a web page contains lots of elements to engage and help visitors. Some elements are more important than others. With the help of the inline CSS, you can highlight certain elements so that they catch the attention of your visitors right away once they reach there. See the following example and try it out.

```
<html>
<body>
<h1>I will tell you a story about an eagle.</h1>
<h2>The is a short story.</h2>
```

```
<p style="color:blue;margin-left:25px;"> Once,
there was an eagle that flew high in the skies,

<br> touching upon the tip of the mountains.

<br> One day she found a ring, stuck in the
branch of an apple tree.

<br> She took it and flew to her nest. While
playing with it, she got her head stuck into it.

<br> She didn't panic and hit her head into the
stump of the tree to get rid of it.

<br> Instead, she embraced it as a mark of
distinction among fellow eagles.

<br> Then one day she drenched her head in oil
and the ring moved out of her neck.</p>

</body>

</html>
```

(How To Add CSS, n.d)

Chapter 3

CSS Margins, Padding, and Width

CSS margin properties allow you to create more space around certain HTML elements that are outside of the defined borders. You can customize margins to suit your webpage. In addition to CSS margins, this chapter will walk you through CSS paddings and adjustment of the width on a CSS style sheet.

You will learn how you can use CSS margins to format the text and make it look good on the web page. There are several values of CSS margins that you can use in the code. Similarly, the chapter will shed light on CSS padding to generate space around a piece of text and headings. This will decrease congestion on your page and make it look smooth.

CSS Margin

Margin can be adjusted from the top, right, bottom, and left. CSS margin properties have the value named as 'auto' by which the browser can calculate the margin. By 'length' value, you can set the margin in cm, px, and pt. When you use % value, you can set the width in terms of percentage. Besides, you can specify the margin by inheriting it from the parent CSS element. You also can add negative values. Let's try to set margin values for different CSS elements.

```
<!DOCTYPE html>
```

```html
<html>
<head>
<style>
div {
   border: 4px solid black;
   margin-top: 80px;
   margin-bottom: 80px;
   margin-right: 80px;
   margin-left: 80px;
   background-color: light blue;
}
</style>
</head>
<body>
<h1>I will tell you a story about an eagle.</h1>
<h2>The story is a short one.</h2>
<p> Once, there was an eagle that flew high in
the skies,
<br> touching upon the tip of the mountains.</p>
<div> One day she found a ring, stuck in the
branch of an apple tree.
<br> She took it and flew to her nest. While
playing with it, she got her head stuck into it.
<br> She didn't panic and hit her head into the
stump of the tree to get rid of it.
<br> Instead, she embraced it as a mark of
distinction among fellow eagles.
```

```
<br> Then one day she drenched her head in oil
and the ring moved out of her neck.</div>

</body>

</html>
```

There is a shorthand property to set the margins using which you can specify all the margin properties in a single line. This is a shorter and faster way to write the code and have results, perfect for seasoned programmers.

```
<!DOCTYPE html>

<html>

<head>

<style>

div {

    border: 4px solid black;

    margin: 80px 80px 80px 80px;

    background-color: light blue;

}

</style>

</head>

<body>

<h1>I will tell you a story about an eagle.</h1>

<h2>The story is a short one.</h2>

<p> Once, there was an eagle that flew high in
the skies,

<br> touching upon the tip of the mountains.

<br> One day she found a ring, stuck in the
branch of an apple tree.
```

```
<br> She took it and flew to her nest. While
playing with it, she got her head stuck into
it.</p>

<div> She didn't panic and hit her head into the
stump of the tree to get rid of it.

<br> Instead, she embraced it as a mark of
distinction among fellow eagles.

<br> Then one day she drenched her head in oil
and the ring moved out of her neck.</div>

</body>

</html>
```

The result will be the same as above. Short-hand property is an interesting property because you can further shorten the code and allow the browser to load it faster. This affects the response from your visitors. The faster the browser loads your web page, the better experience your visitors will have. So, there are likely to come again on your website. Put yourself in a similar condition. You might have come across lots of web pages on the internet, which wouldn't just load before burning a full minute. Did you feel frustrated or annoyed? Did you ever visit the same website again, no matter how direly you needed the information it had got? Even if a website has put everything in their e-commerce store on a hot sale, you will not drop the idea of buying anything if the webpage doesn't load faster.

Just imagine if you have decided to open an e-commerce store to sell Nike shoes. Nikes shoes are always hot in demand across the world. You might not pay much attention to the design of your website, believing that the popularity and quality of the product in your store will take care of everything else, but you are wrong. Only a handful of users will wait for your page to load. Bad for business! So, it is a good idea to learn and use short-hand property in different CSS style codes.

```
<!DOCTYPE html>
<html>
<head>
<style>
div {
   border: 4px solid black;
   margin: 150px 100px 150px;
   background-color: light blue;
}
</style>
</head>
<body>
<h1>I will tell you a story about an eagle.</h1>
<h2>The story is a short one.</h2>
<p> Once, there was an eagle that flew high in
the skies,
<br> touching upon the tip of the mountains.
<br> One day she found a ring, stuck in the
branch of an apple tree. </p>
<div> She took it and flew to her nest. While
playing with it, she got her head stuck into it.
<br> She didn't panic and hit her head into the
stump of the tree to get rid of it.
<br> Instead, she embraced it as a mark of
distinction among fellow eagles.
```

```
<br> Then one day she drenched her head in oil
and the ring moved out of her neck.</div>
</body>
</html>
```

Although I have put in just three values, yet the browser will read them as four. The value in the center will be treated as left as well as right margins. Similarly, you can shorten it to two.

```
<!DOCTYPE html>
<html>
<head>
<style>
div {
    border: 4px solid black;
    margin: 150px 150px;
    background-color: light blue;
}
</style>
</head>
<body>
<h1>I will tell you a story about an eagle.</h1>
<h2>The story is a short one.</h2>
<p> Once, there was an eagle that flew high in
the skies,
<br> touching upon the tip of the mountains.
<br> One day she found a ring, stuck in the
branch of an apple tree. </p>
```

```
<div> She took it and flew to her nest. While
playing with it, she got her head stuck into it.
<br> She didn't panic and hit her head into the
stump of the tree to get rid of it.
<br> Instead, she embraced it as a mark of
distinction among fellow eagles.
<br> Then one day she drenched her head in oil
and the ring moved out of her neck.</div>
</body>
</html>
```

In this code, the first value will be allocated to top and bottom margins while the second value will be allocated to the right and left margins. So, that's how you can further shorten the code, but it is only possible if you

The Auto Value

As I have already discussed in the introduction of this chapter, CSS margin property can be set to auto to centralize an element in a horizontal position within the container. The auto value allows you to save time during coding, which you would have spent on adjusting the margins. This feature will make your coding appear smart and smooth. Let's see how to set the margin property to auto.

```
<!DOCTYPE html>
<html>
<head>
<style>
div {
   Width: 200px;
```

```
    border: 4px solid green;

    margin: auto;

    background-color: light blue;

}

</style>

</head>

<body>

<h1>I will tell you a story about an eagle.</h1>

<h2>The story is a short one.</h2>

<p> Once, there was an eagle that flew high in
the skies,

<br> touching upon the tip of the mountains.

<br> One day she found a ring, stuck in the
branch of an apple tree. </p>

<div> She took it and flew to her nest. While
playing with it, she got her head stuck into it.

<br> She didn't panic and hit her head into the
stump of the tree to get rid of it.

<br> Instead, she embraced it as a mark of
distinction among fellow eagles.

<br> Then one day she drenched her head in oil
and the ring moved out of her neck.</div>

</body>

</html>
```

The Inherit Value

CSS is amazing if we want to diversify codes, simply them, and manipulate their usage. The inherit value for the margin property is yet another feature which can make writing codes simple and easy. You can inherit the margin value from the parent element and use it in other margin properties. That's how you will not have to set an individual value for each margin property. The code example for the inherit value is stated as under. You can read it, analyze it and use it in a code editor as it is or altering it as per your choice. Save it then and open it in a browser to see the result.

```
<!DOCTYPE html>
<html>
<head>
<style>
div {
   border: 4px solid green;
   margin-left: 80px;
   background-color: light blue;
}
p.one {
    margin-left: inherit;
}
</style>
</head>
<body>
<h1>I will tell you a story about an eagle.</h1>
<h2>The story is a short one.</h2>
<p class="one"> Once, there was an eagle that flew high in the skies,
<br> touching upon the tip of the mountains.
```

```
<br> One day she found a ring, stuck in the
branch of an apple tree.</p>

<div> She took it and flew to her nest. While
playing with it, she got her head stuck in it.

<br> She didn't panic or hit her head on the
stump of a tree to get rid of it.

<br> Instead, she embraced it as a mark of
distinction among fellow eagles.

<br>Then, one day she drenched her head in oil
and the ring came off of her neck.</div>

</body>

</html>
```

Sometimes you might feel that the margin which you have put in an HTML element has been collapsed. Top and bottom margins usually get collapsed and are displayed as a single margin. This single margin stands equal to the bigger of the two margins. Margin collapse happens only to the top and bottom margins and doesn't affect the left and right margins. In the next example, I will create a document without margin property; then, I will add a margin and see how they get collapsed.

```
<!DOCTYPE html>

<html>

<body>

<h1>I will tell you a story about an eagle.</h1>

<h2>The story is a short one.</h2>

<p> Once upon a time there was an eagle.</p>

<div> One day she found a ring stuck in a branch
of an Apple tree.<br> She took it and flew
toward her nest<br> that was at the top of a
```

pine tree.
 To sort out what this thing is, <br> she got her head stuck into it.
 She didn't hit her head in the stump of the tree to get rid of it.
 Instead, she embraced it as a mark of distinction among fellow eagles.
 The eagle community started envying her.
 One day she drenched her head in oil and the ring moved out of her neck.</div>

```
</body>
</html>
```

I encourage you to try out this example in the code editor you are using so that you can tell the difference when you compare it with the results of the next code example. Now in the following code example, I am going to add margins to see how they get collapsed. Also, take this code, save it in the editor, and see the difference in the browser window.

```
<!DOCTYPE html>
<html>
<head>
<style>
h1 {
  margin: 0 0 100px 0;
}
h2 {
    margin: 50px 0 0 0;
}
</style>
</head>
```

```
<body>

<h1>I will tell you a story about an eagle.</h1>

<h2>The story is a short one.</h2>

<p> Once, there was an eagle that flew high in
the skies,

<br> touching upon the tip of the mountains.

<br> One day she found a ring, stuck in the
branch of an apple tree.

<br>She took it and flew to her nest. While
playing with it, she got her head stuck in
it.</p>

<div> She didn't panic or hit her head on the
stump of a tree to get rid of it.

<br> Instead, she embraced it as a mark of
distinction among fellow eagles.

<br>Then, one day she drenched her head in oil
and the ring came off of her neck.</div>

</body>

</html>
```

(CSS Margins, n.d)

CSS Padding

Why do we use CSS programming on our website? To make them appear beautiful and attractive. CSS padding property adds neatness to the headlines and paragraphs. If your visitors feel congested when they are looking at your web page, they are unlikely to revisit your website. You have to offer them a sense of spaciousness that you need to learn and include CSS padding property in your code.

The CSS padding property is generally used to add extra space around the content of HTML elements. The spacing is added inside the borders of the HTML element. CSS padding property gives you full control over the size of the spacing, and you can set it individually for the topside, the left and right sides, and the bottom side.

Certain values can be added to the padding property. These properties include length, inherit, and percentage value. With length value, you can specify padding in cm, px, and pt. The percentage property specifies padding in terms of percentages. The inherit value tends to specify padding that can be inherited from the parent element. You cannot add negative values in the padding property.

```
<!DOCTYPE html>
<html>
<head>
<style>
div {
    border: 2px solid green;
    background-color: light blue;
    padding-top: 75px;
    padding-right: 20px;
    padding-bottom: 50px;
    padding-left: 75px;
}
</style>
</head>
<body>
```

```
<h1>I will tell you a story about an eagle.</h1>
<h2>The story is a short one.</h2>
<p> Once, there was an eagle that flew high in
the skies,
<br> touching upon the tip of the mountains.
<br> One day she found a ring, stuck in the
branch of an apple tree.</p>
<div>She took it and flew to her nest. While
playing with it, she got her head stuck in it.
<br>She didn't panic or hit her head on the
stump of a tree to get rid of it.
<br>One day she drenched her head in oil and the
ring came off of her neck.</div>
</body>
</html>
```

Like all the other CSS properties, CSS padding offers users great diversity. You can adjust the values as per your requirements and liking. In the next code example, I will decrease the values of padding. Let's see how you can change it and get different results.

```
<!DOCTYPE html>
<html>
<head>
<style>
div {
    border: 2px solid green;
    background-color: light blue;
    padding-top: 25px;
    padding-right: 20px;
```

```
      padding-bottom: 20px;

      padding-left: 25px;

}

</style>

</head>

<body>

<h1>I will tell you a story of an eagle.</h1>

<h2>This is a short story.</h2>

<p> Once, there was an eagle that flew high in
the skies,

<br> touching upon the tip of the mountains.

<br> One day she found a ring, stuck in the
branch of an apple tree.</p>

<div>She took it and flew to her nest. While
playing with it, she got her head stuck in it.

<br>She didn't panic or hit her head on the
stump of a tree to get rid of it.

<br>One day she drenched her head in oil and the
ring came off of her neck.</div>

</body>

</html>
```

Like margin, padding also has shorthand property. You can shorten the code by writing all the values in a single line. As I have explained earlier on in the margin property, the main goal behind using CSS padding property is to cut down on the time which is consumed on writing the code and to facilitate the browser so that it can read the code quickly thus loads it quickly. Let's move on to the example.

```
<!DOCTYPE html>
<html>
<head>
<style>
div {
   border: 2px solid green;
   background-color: light blue;
   padding-top: 25px 50px 50 px 50px


}
</style>
</head>
<body>
<h1>I will tell you a story about an eagle.</h1>
<h2>The story is a short one.</h2>
<p class="one"> Once, there was an eagle that
flew high in the skies,
<br> touching upon the tip of the mountains.
<br> One day she found a ring, stuck in the
branch of an apple tree.</p>
<div>She took it and flew to her nest. While
playing with it, she got her head stuck in it.
<br>She didn't panic or hit her head on the
stump of a tree to get rid of it.
<br>One day she drenched her head in oil and the
ring came off of her neck.</div>
</body>
</html>
```

As with margins, you can merge up values of padding. If you cut them down to three, the value in the center will represent the right and left paddings. If you cut them down to two, the first will represent the top and bottom padding, and the second will represent the left and right padding. That's how you can further shorten the code and speed up the page loading time. The code example is as under.

```
<!DOCTYPE html>
<html>
<head>
<style>
div {
    border: 2px solid green;
    padding: 100px 150px 100px;
    background-color: light blue;
}
</style>
</head>
<body>
<h1> I will tell you a story about an eagle.</h1>
<h2> The story is a short one.</h2>
<p> Once, there was an eagle that flew high in the skies,
<br> touching upon the tip of the mountains.
<br> One day she found a ring, stuck in the branch of an apple tree. </p>
```

```
<div>She took it and flew to her nest. While
playing with it, she got her head stuck in it.
<br>She didn't panic or hit her head on the
stump of a tree to get rid of it.
<br>Then, one day she drenched her head in oil
and the ring came off of her neck.</div>
</body>
</html>
```

Please run the above code example in the code editor, which in my case is Notepad, ++, save it, and then move on to open the file in the Internet browser. Now I am going to slash the third one as well and leave the code with two padding values. Just like the margin property, the browser will read it as four. Let's see how it is done.

```
<!DOCTYPE html>
<html>
<head>
<style>
div {
    padding: 50px 100px;
    background-color: white;
    font-size: 30px
}
</style>
</head>
<body>
<h1>I will tell you a story about an eagle.</h1>
<h2>This is a short story.</h2>
```

```
<p> Once, there was an eagle that flew high in
the skies,

<br> touching upon the tip of the mountains.

<br> One day she found a ring, stuck in the
branch of an apple tree.</p>

<div>She took it and flew to her nest. While
playing with it, she got her head stuck in it.

<br>She didn't panic or hit her head on the
stump of a tree to get rid of it.

<br>One day she drenched her head in oil and the
ring came off of her neck.</div>

</body>

</html>
```

(CSS Padding, n.d)

One important change that I made besides the padding values is the elimination of the border and changing the background color to white. You can see changes in the code and also run it in the editor. If you want to change it back, you can add the border property in the code. More on CSS borders will come in the next chapter. The interesting thing is that you can create the code with just one value in the padding property. Still, the browser will take it as four and apply it on the four sides of the paragraph. Let's try it out.

```
<!DOCTYPE html>

<html>

<head>

<style>

div {
   padding: 50px;
```

```
    background-color: white;
    font-size: 20px
}
</style>
</head>
```

I have deliberately shortened the code to save some space. You can take the body of the code from the previous example and add it up to the tail of the current code. Take this sample to the coding editor and then copy the body and paste it on the tail of the code. Now run the code and see the results in the browser. The single value, which I have put in the padding property, will be applied on all the four sides of the paragraph.

CSS width property specifies the width of the content area of an HTML element. A content area can be defined as the portion in the padding, margin, and border areas of the element. If you have specified the width of an element, the padding you will add to it will be a part of the total width of that element. An example code will help you understand easily.

```
<!DOCTYPE html>
<html>
<head>
<style>
div.one {
    width: 400px;
    background-color: pink;
    font-size: 20px;
}
```

```
div.two {

    width: 400px;

    padding: 40px;

    background-color: light blue;

}
</style>
</head>
<body>
<h1>I will tell you a story about an eagle.</h1>
<h2> The story is a short one.</h2>
<div class="one"> Once, there was an eagle that
flew high in the skies,
<br> touching upon the tip of the mountains.
<br> One day she found a ring, stuck in the
branch of an apple tree. </div>
<div class="two"> She took it and flew to her
nest. While playing with it, she got her head
stuck in it.
<br>She didn't panic or hit her head on the
stump of a tree to get rid of it.
<br>One day she drenched her head in oil and the
ring came off of her neck.</div>
</body>
</html>
```

The box-sizing property can help us build CSS layouts in a faster and easier way. It adds to them the intuitive element. The problem starts rising when we the width as well as the length of our content go out of the window when we start adding the border and padding property to an HTML element.

There are generally three possible values for CSS box sizing, namely, content-box, border-box, and padding-box. The most popular of them is border-box. I have used the same in the example, which is given below. The box sizing: the border-box property is supported by mainly all the current versions of major Internet browsers such as Firefox, Google Chrome, and Opera.

The other two versions of box sizing such as padding-box are only supported by a handful of browsers. For example, padding-box only runs on Firefox. Even border-box property is not recognized by the older versions of Internet explorer 8 and the older versions.

```
<!DOCTYPE html>
<html>
<head>
<style>
div {
   width: 300px;
   padding: 40px;
   font-size: 15px;
   box-sizing: border-box;
}
</style>
</head>
<body>
<h1>I will tell you a story about an eagle.</h1>
```

```
<p> Once, there was an eagle that flew high in
the skies,

<br> touching upon the tip of the mountains.

<br> One day she found a ring, stuck in the
branch of an apple tree.</p>

<div>She took it and flew to her nest. While
playing with it, she got her head stuck in it.

<br>She didn't panic or hit her head on the
stump of a tree to get rid of it.

<br>One day she drenched her head in oil and the
ring came off of her neck.</div>

</body>

</html>
```

(CSS Padding, n.d)

CSS Height and Weight

In CSS, there are dedicated width and height properties, which you can use to set the height and width of HTML elements as per your choice. The width and height properties don't include margins, padding, and borders. Like margins and paddings, CSS height and weight also offer some values. The first is 'auto,' which tells the browser to set the height and width value at the default values. The second is length using which you will have to define the height as well as width in cm and px. The third is the percentage for which you have to define the height and width in terms of percentage. The fourth is 'initial' for which you can set the height and width at default. The final is inherit using which you can inherit the height and width values that you have allocated to the parent value.

```html
<!DOCTYPE html>
<html>
<head>
<style>
div {
    height: 100px;
    width: 50%;
    background-color: light blue;
}
</style>
</head>
<body>
<h1> I will tell you a story about an
eagle.</h1>
<h2> The story is a short one.</h2>
<p> Once, there was an eagle that flew high in
the skies,
<br> touching upon the tip of the mountains.
<br> One day she found a ring, stuck in the
branch of an apple tree.</p>
<div>She took it and flew to her nest. While
playing with it, she got her head stuck in it.
<br>She didn't panic or hit her head on the
stump of a tree to get rid of it.
<br>One day she drenched her head in oil and the
ring came off of her neck.</div>
</body>
</html>
```

Please take the above written code and run it on the Internet browser. You will be able to see a half filled text. It happened because I didn't put in the right values for height and width that could perfectly enclose the piece of text from all possible ends. In the next code I'll rectify what I did wrong. You can use the corrected code to see what difference it will have on the result.

```
<!DOCTYPE html>
<html>
<head>
<style>
div {
   height: 180px;
   width: 50%;
   background-color: light blue;
}
</style>
</head>
```

I have deliberately slashed the body of the code to save some space. When you have written the above snippet of code in the editor, take the body from the previous example and run it in the editor to get the result. Also, don't just rely on what I have written in the code. You can go the extra mile to fill it in with different other values and see what results you have. This is how you will get to know what width and height can work for your web page.

When you are on your way to building your first web page, you will have to try multiple height and width features before reaching the perfect size. The above code, snippet, carries a short story. Imagine a website which published short children stories. As these stories are short, you will have to publish a set of four or six on the web page to engage the visitors. At that point, you will have to reach the perfect width and height for all the four HTML elements so that they may appear attractive.

One important thing that you should note is that the height and weight properties of CSS don't include margins padding and border. They tend to set the height and width of what is inside the margin, padding, and border of the element. That's the tricky part of CSS. You have to reach the right values for height and width properties so that they pair up well with other CSS properties.

Chapter 4

CSS Borders, Background, etc...

One interesting thing to learn about CSS is that you can add border to headings and paragraphs to make them look better. The CSS border properties allow you to specify what kind of style, width as well as color you need for the border of an HTML element. This chapter will also walk you through CSS background properties.

The background of your web page matters much because it affects the visibility and readability of the text. If the background color scheme is right, your visitors will likely extend their stay on your website. If you the color scheme bothers their eyes, their stay on your website will cut to half.

```
<html>
<body>
<h1 style="border:2px solid Tomato;">I will tell
you a story about an eagle.</h1>
<h2>This is a short story.</h2>
<p style="border:2px solid Violet;"> Once, there
was an eagle that flew high in the skies,
<br> touching upon the tip of the mountains.
<br> One day she found a ring, stuck in the
branch of an apple tree.</p>
</body>
```

```
</html>
```

In the above code example, I have added the border properties inside the lines of codes. I have set the thickness of the border at 2px for both HTML elements. The colors are different for both. One important thing to remember is that you don't have to add a separate color property to specify the color of the borders. Just place them inside after the values for thickness, and the browser will read it. Try out the above-mentioned code example and see the results. Do some experiments such as changing the colors of the borders to light blue or pink or gray or whatever touches your heart.

It is always better to have a comprehensive survey of your target audience. For example, for a website which publishes short stories for the children, you can take the liberty to add lots of colors because children love colors. Even if parents are visiting your website to pick up stories for their kids, still the choice of colors should be kept in check. Try out bright colors as they will lift the design of your website and make it distinct among your competitors.

Similarly, if you are building a website which will offer career advice to graduates, you should go for more decent colors such as gray, brown, light brown and yellow. So, really depends on the content. Borders can be created in a wide range of designs depending on your choice and requirements. Let's try to create borders in three different styles. I will add different border styles to h1, h2 and p on my web page. Let's see the code.

```
<html>
<body>
<style>
```

```
h1.dashed {border-style: dashed;}

h2.mix {border-style: solid dashed dotted
double;}

p.ridge {border-style: ridge;}

</style>

<h1 class="dashed">I will tell you a story about
an eagle.</h1>

<h2 class="mix">This a short story.</h2>

<p class="ridge"> Once, there was an eagle that
flew high in the skies,

<br> touching upon the tip of the mountains.

<br> One day she found a ring, stuck in the
branch of an apple tree.</p>

<p>She took it and flew to her nest. While
playing with it, she got her head stuck in it.

<br>She didn't panic or hit her head on the
stump of a tree to get rid of it.

<br>One day she drenched her head in oil and the
ring came off of her neck.</p>

</body>

</html>
```

You can see in the above code that I have added three different border designs to different HTML elements, which include dashed, dotted and ridged. We also can try out other designs as well. Let's give you a taste of some other designs as well.

```
<html>

<body>

<style>
```

```
h1.outset {border-style: outset;}

h2.inset {border-style: inset;}

p.double {border-style: double;}

</style>

<h1 class="outset">I will tell you a story about
an eagle.</h1>

<h2 class="inset">This is a short story for
little kids.</h2>

<p class="double"> Once, there was an eagle that
flew high in the skies,

<br> touching upon the tip of the mountains.

<br> One day she found a ring, stuck in the
branch of an apple tree.</p>

</body>

</html>
```

CSS Border Width

CSS borders have a width property to decide the thickness of the border on your web page. You can set the width in px to make it thick, thin, and medium. Also, you can add different width sizes for headings and paragraphs. Width matters. The thickness level I have used in the example code is high. This was just to make them visible enough so that you can notice them.

When you start building a page, you will have to adjust the size to suit your needs. After all, that much thick border will hardly look any better on a live website unless it has a purpose. For example, if you have to make an announcement on your website about an upcoming event or Spring Sale, you can use a thick border to catch the attention of your visitors. Otherwise, make it slim and smart.

Let's see the code example for that.

```
<html>
<body>
<style>
h1{
     border-style: outset;
     border-color: green;
     border-width: 20px;
}
h2{
     border-style: dashed;
     border-color: violet;
     border-width: 10px;
}
p.one{
     border-style: inset;
     border-color: blue;
     border-width: 10px;
}
p.two{
     border-style: double;
     border-color: red;
     border-width: 10px;
}
```

```
</style>

<h1 class="h1">I will tell you a story about an
eagle.</h1>

<h2 class="h2">The story is a short one.</h2>

<p class="one"> Once, there was an eagle that
flew high in the skies,

<br> touching upon the tip of the mountains.

<br> One day she found a ring, stuck in the
branch of an apple tree.</p>

<p>She took it and flew to her nest. While
playing with it, she got her head stuck in it.

<br>She didn't panic or hit her head on the
stump of a tree to get rid of it.

<br>One day she drenched her head in oil and the
ring came off of her neck.</p>

</body>

</html>
```

> Once, there was an eagle that flew high in the skies,
>
> touching upon the tip of the mountains.
>
> One day she found a ring stuck in the branch of an apple tree.

She took it and flew to her nest. While playing with it, she got her head stuck in it.

She didn't panic or hit her head on the stump of a tree to get rid of it.

One day she drenched her head in oil and the ring came off of her neck.

Let's try to give different styles to a single border in the code below.

```
<html>
<body>
<style>
p.two{
     border-top-style: double;
     border-left-style: outset;
     border-bottom-style: inset;
     border-right-style: solid;
}
</style>
<h1>I will tell you a story about an eagle.</h1>
<h2>This is a short story for little kids.</h2>
<p class="two"> Once, there was an eagle that
flew high in the skies,
<br> touching upon the tip of the mountains.
<br> One day she found a ring, stuck in the
branch of an apple tree.
<p>She took it and flew to her nest. While
playing with it, she got her head stuck in it.
<br>She didn't panic or hit her head on the
stump of a tree to get rid of it.
<br>One day she drenched her head in oil and the
ring came off of her neck.</p>
</body>
</html>
```

(CSS Borders, n.d)

63

CSS Backgrounds

CSS background properties are used to define the background effects for different HTML elements. There is a wide range of background properties that you can use to add spice to your web page. These properties are about attachment, image, color, and position. We will discuss them one by one to have a clear understanding of each of them. Background is an important part of a web page. The shading and style of the background affect the entire page and content like text, headings, and tables. If the color that you have selected for background turns out to be a bad choice, the web page can be just illegible. So, choose wisely. I will take the same HTML document that I have been using to apply the background property. Let's jump to Notepad++.

```
<html>
<body>
<style>
p.two{
    background-color: gray;
}
h1 {
    background-color: pink;
}
p.one {
    background-color: orange;
}
h2 {
    background-color: violet;
```

```
}
</style>
<h1>I will tell you a story about an eagle.</h1>
<h2>This is a short story.</h2>
<p class="one"> Once, there was an eagle that
flew high in the skies,
<br> touching upon the tip of the mountains.
<br> One day she found a ring, stuck in the
branch of an apple tree.</p>
<p class="two">She took it and flew to her nest.
While playing with it, she got her head stuck in
it.
<br>She didn't panic or hit her head on the
stump of a tree to get rid of it.
<br>One day she drenched her head in oil and the
ring came off of her neck.</p>
</body>
</html>
```

You can take this code example and run it in the browser. Change the colors of the background to see different results. You can notice that I have used the class method to style the background of different elements. The method enabled me to style the headings and multiple paragraphs in a single snippet of code. If this example has to be displayed as a homepage on your website, you have to be careful about background colors. Usually, homepages carry lots of details to engage the visitor once it lands on your website. Suppose you have to integrate a kind of sales ad copy to your website. You have got the draft ready. Everything from sentence structure to word usage is pretty fine except one thing. Your visitors are not engaging with the sales ad, and you can tell that from the fact that your sales are stagnant.

You keep thinking about what is the problem until you ask your friend about the sales ad which you have put on the website to seek advice, and he asks you when did you out that sales ad on the website because he didn't notice anything new when he visited the website the other day. It is only then that you realize that how anyone could detect it when there was no distinction between usual content and the sales ad. You should throw some colors in the background of that sales ad. If you want to style a specific part of the web page, too, you can change the background by another method. Let's see how to do that.

```
<html>
<body>
<style>
div{
    background-color: gray;
}
h1 {
    background-color: pink;
}
h2 {
    background-color: violet;
}
</style>
<h1>I will tell you a story about an eagle.</h1>
<h2>This is a short story.</h2>
```

```
<p> Once, there was an eagle that flew high in
the skies,

<br> touching upon the tip of the mountains.

<br> One day she found a ring, stuck in the
branch of an apple tree. </p>

<div>She took it and flew to her nest. While
playing with it, she got her head stuck in it.

<br>She didn't panic or hit her head on the
stump of a tree to get rid of it.

<br>One day she drenched her head in oil and the
ring came off of her neck.</div>

</body>

</html>
```

Chapter 5

CSS Texts

The way your text appears before the reader affects your sales or overall ranking in search engines. You want your visitors to stay on your page for a while; that's why your page should look good, and also it should be easy to read. You have to decide the style of your font, the color, the spacing between words, lines and paragraphs. Let's go on to analyze different types of fonts that you can use. There are two types of font-family names. The first is the generic family, which is a group of font families that have a similar look, such as Monospace as well as Serif. The other type is font family that is a specific font family like Arial as well as Times New Roman.

```
<html>
<head>
<title>I will tell you a story about an
eagle.</title>
<style type="text/css">
body {
    font-family: serif, Georgia, Times:}
    .credits {
font-family: Courier, monospace;}
</style>
```

```
</head>

<body>

<p class="credits"> Once, there was an eagle
that flew high in the skies,

<br> touching upon the tip of the mountains.

<br> One day she found a ring, stuck in the
branch of an apple tree.

<br> She took it and flew to her nest. While
playing with it, she got her head stuck in it.

<br> She didn't panic or hit her head on the
stump of a tree to get rid of it.

<br> Then, one day she drenched her head in oil
and the ring came off of her neck.</p>

</body>

</html>
```

You can specify the typeface that can be used for any piece of text
which is inside the element on which you are applying the CSS rule.
Different users have different typefaces installed on their operating
systems; that's why you need to include a variety of typefaces so that
your users can see the page in the typeface that they have installed
even if that typeface is not your first choice. I have specified a list of
fonts that you can see separated by commas in the code. It is always
a good choice to put a generic font size that is common on different
operating systems. You have to put the font size in double-quotes
that consist of more than one number.

Font-Size

The font-size makes you capable of specifying the size of the text.
The most common way is to decide upon the font-size in pixels.

They allow you to have greater control over the space the text has to take up. You can specify it by the letters px. The other way to decide upon the font-size is to set is in percentage. By default, the font-size in your browser is 16px. In this parameter, the size of 75% will be equivalent to 12 px, and 200% will be equivalent to 32 px.

```
<html>
<head>
<style type="text/css">
h1 {
     font-family: serif, Georgia, Times;
     font-size: 100px; }
h2 {
     font-famlity: Verdana, Cambria, sans-serif;
     font-size: 50px; }
     .credits {
     font-family: Courier, monospace;
     font-size: 30px; }
</style>
</head>
<body>
<h1>Let me tell you a story.</h1>
<h2>The story is a short one.</h2>
<p class="credits"> Once, there was an eagle
that flew high in the skies,
<br> touching upon the tip of the mountains.
<br> One day she found a ring, stuck in the
branch of an apple tree.
```

```
<br> She took it and flew to her nest. While
playing with it, she got her head stuck in it.
<br> She didn't panic or hit her head on the
stump of a tree to get rid of it.
<br> Instead, she embraced it as a mark of
distinction among fellow eagles.
<br> Then, one day she drenched her head in oil
and the ring came off of her neck.</p>
</body>
</html>
```

See how your browser will display the same code.

Let me tell you a story.

The story is a short one.

```
Once, there was an eagle that
flew high in the skies,
touching upon the tip of the
mountains.
One day she found a ring stuck
in the branch of an apple tree.
```

She took it and flew to her nest. While playing with it, she got her head stuck into it.
She didn't panic and hit her head into the stump of the tree to get rid of it.
One day she drenched her head in oil, and the ring moved out of her neck.

There can be a slight difference in the display as per the type of the browser, which you have been using. In the above code, I have specified different font sizes for h1, h2, and paragraph elements of HTML. You can see that I have used px to decide the font size of different pieces of texts. Now we will try to fix the font size by using the percentage technique. Let's see how to do that.

```
<html>
<head>
<style type="text/css">
h1 {
    font-family: serif, Georgia, Times;
    font-size: 200%;}
h2 {
    font-famlity: Verdana, Cambria, sans-serif;
    font-size: 150%;}
    .credits {
```

```
      font-family: Courier, monospace;
      font-size: 75%; }
</style>
</head>
<body>
<h1>Let me tell you a story.</h1>
<h2>The story is a short one.</h2>
<p class="credits"> Once, there was an eagle
that flew high in the skies,
<br> touching upon the tip of the mountains.
<br> One day she found a ring, stuck in the
branch of an apple tree.
<br> She took it and flew to her nest. While
playing with it, she got her head stuck into it.
<br> She didn't panic and hit her head into the
stump of the tree to get rid of it.
<br> One day she drenched her head in oil and
the ring moved out of her neck.</p>
</body>
</html>
```

The percentage property works as well as the px property. Let's see the result.

Let me tell you a story.

The story is a short one.

```
Once, there was an eagle that flew high in the skies,
touching upon the tip of the mountains.
One day she found a ring stuck in the branch of an apple
```

```
tree.
She took it and flew to her nest. While playing with it, she
got her head stuck in it.

She didn't panic or hit her head on the stump of a tree to
get rid of it.

Then, one day she drenched her head in oil and the ring came
off of her neck.
```

(Duckett, 2011)

There is a third technique for deciding upon the font size: the EMS technique. An em matches the width of a letter m. With the help of EMS, you can change the size of a piece of text in relation to the size of the text that exists in the parent element.

```html
<html>
<head>
<style type="text/css">
h1 {
    font-family: serif, Georgia, Times;
    font-size: 1.5em; }
h2 {
    font-famlity: Verdana, Cambria, sans-serif;
    font-size: 1.3em; }
    .credits {
    font-family: Courier, monospace;
    font-size: 0.74em; }
</style>
</head>
<body>
```

```
<h1>Let me tell you a story of an eagle.</h1>
<p class="credits"> Once, there was an eagle
that flew high in the skies,
<br> touching upon the tip of the mountains.
<br> One day she found a ring, stuck in the
branch of an apple tree.
<br> She took it and flew to her nest. While
playing with it, she got her head stuck in it.
<br> She didn't panic or hit her head on the
stump of a tree to get rid of it.
<br> Instead, she embraced it as a mark of
distinction among fellow eagles.
<br> Then, one day she drenched her head in oil
and the ring came off of her neck.</p>
</body>
</html>
```

(Duckett, 2011)

Font-Style

This CSS property is used for specification of italic text. You can add three values to this property. The first is 'normal' which displays the text normally. The second is 'italic' which displays the text in italics. The third is 'leaning' which appears similar to italic but is less supported than that. Let's try them out on our web page.

```
<html>
<head>
<style type="text/css">
h1.normal {
```

```
    font-family: serif, Georgia, Times;

    font-size: 1.5em;

    font-style: normal;

}

h2 {

    font-family: Verdana, Cambria, sans-serif;

    font-size: 1.3em;

    font-style: oblique;

}

    p.credits {

    font-family: Courier, monospace;

    font-size: 1em;

    font-style: italic;

    }

    p.two {

    font-family: Courier, monospace;

    font-size: 1em;

    font-style: normal;

</style>

</head>

<body>

<h2 class="oblique">This is a short story.</h2>

<p class="credits"> Once, there was an eagle
that flew high in the skies,

<br> touching upon the tip of the mountains.

<br> One day she found a ring, stuck in the
branch of an apple tree.</p>
```

```
<p class="two">She took it and flew to her nest.
While playing with it, she got her head stuck in
it.

<br>She didn't panic or hit her head on the
stump of a tree to get rid of it.

<br>One day she drenched her head in oil and the
ring came off of her neck.</p>

</body>

</html>
```

This is a short story.

Once, there was an eagle that flew high in the skies,
touching upon the tip of the mountains.
One day she found a ring stuck in the branch of an apple tree.

```
She took it and flew to her nest. While playing
with it, she got her head stuck in it.

She didn't panic or hit her head on the stump of a
tree to get rid of it.

Then, one day she drenched her head in oil and the
ring came off of her neck.
```

Observe the variety of font-styles in the example. I have added three different font-styles to different parts of the web page. You can see how normal, oblique, and italic is displayed on the web page. Don't forget to mention the class name to get it right.

Font Weight

Another important thing to remember about the font-size is that you can easily set the weight of the font when it comes to forming CSS property. You can set it to normal, bold, light, or thicker as suit your requirements. I am going to add font-weight to our web page. Let's see how the browser treats it.

```
<html>
<head>
<style type="text/css">
h1.normal {
    font-family: serif, Georgia, Times;
    font-size: 1.5em;
    font-style: normal;
    font-weight: normal;
}
h2 {
    font-family: Verdana, Cambria, sans-serif;
    font-size: 1.3em;
    font-style: oblique;
    font-weight: lighter
}
    p.credits {
    font-family: Courier, monospace;
    font-size: 1em;
    font-style: italic;
    font-weight: bold;
```

```
      }
      p.two {
      font-family: Courier, monospace;
      font-size: 1em;
      font-style: normal;
      font-weight: 900;
</style>
</head>
<body>
<h1>Let me tell you a story about an eagle.</h1>
<h2 class="oblique">This is a short story.</h2>
<p class="credits"> Once, there was an eagle
that flew high in the skies,
<br> touching upon the tip of the mountains.
<br> One day she found a ring, stuck in the
branch of an apple tree.</p>
<p class="two">She took it and flew to her nest.
While playing with it, she got her head stuck in
it.
<br>She didn't panic or hit her head on the
stump of a tree to get rid of it.
<br>One day she drenched her head in oil and the
ring came off of her neck.</p>
</body>
</html>
```

Take the example and get the output in the Internet browser. If you observe closely, you will realize that the font weight started as light and went on getting thicker down the line of code.

In addition to adjusting the font-weight as per your personalized requirements, you can make your font-size responsive so that it can adjust itself according to the device that the visitor on your website is using. It can be a mobile, a computer or a tablet so the font-weight should be responsive to each of them. Let's see how to do that.

```html
<html>
<meta name="viewport" content="width=device-width, initial-scale=1.0">
<body>
<h1 style="font-size:10vw;"> Let me tell you a story.</h1>
<h2 style="font-size:5vw;"> The story is a short one.</h2>
<p style="font-size:5vw;"> Once, there was an eagle that flew high in the skies,
<br> touching upon the tip of the mountains.
<br> One day she found a ring, stuck in the branch of an apple tree.</p>
<p style="font-size:5vw;">She took it and flew to her nest. While playing with it, she got her head stuck in it.
<br>She didn't panic or hit her head on the stump of a tree to get rid of it.
<br>One day she drenched her head in oil and the ring came off of her neck.</p>
</body>
</html>
```

In the above code example, I have used the vw unit to fix the size of font that may appear to you contradictory to my earlier lessons, where I used px and percentages to decide upon the font-size. 10vw means that you are setting the font-size to 10% of the width of the viewport. You have to use it when you are fixing the font-size to match the requirements of the browser. Similarly, 1vw will be 1% of the viewport width. Viewport is the size of the browser window.

Last but not least is the inclusion of font-variant in your CSS rules. The font-variant property tends to specify whether you want a text to be displayed in small caps or not. If you set it to be displayed in small caps, all lowercase letters in the text will be converted to uppercase letters.

```html
<html>
<head>
<style>
h1.small {
    font-variant: small-caps;
}
p.one {
    font-variant: normal;
}
p.two {
    font-variant: small-caps;
}
</style>
</head>
<body>
<h1 class="small">Let me tell you a story.</h1>
```

```
<h2>The story is a short one.</h2>

<p class="one"> Once, there was an eagle that
flew high in the skies,

<br> touching upon the tip of the mountains.

<br> One day she found a ring, stuck in the
branch of an apple tree.</p>

<p class="two">She took it and flew to her nest.
While playing with it, she got her head stuck in
it.

<br>She didn't panic or hit her head on the
stump of a tree to get rid of it.

<br>One day she drenched her head in oil and the
ring came off of her neck.</p>

</body>

</html>
```

(CSS Fonts, n.d)

Chapter 6

CSS Colors

Colors bring joy and meaning to our lives, and similarly, they bring meaning to the web pages as well. This chapter will walk you through the process of specifying colors on your web page. You will get to know about the color terminology because there are so many terms that will aid you when you are going to fill in different colors on your web page. There is a great diversity of colors to choose from. I have already given you a taste of how colors can be integrated into texts and backgrounds. This chapter will take you to the deep end of how things go on.

CSS has a dedicated color property that you can use to specify the colors of the text inside of HTML elements. Up till now, we have learned how to specify colors in HTML documents by simply writing the name of a particular color. Now we will learn other methods to fill in the web page with different colors.

One of these methods is putting in RGB values. These values tend to express colors by giving you the freedom to decide how much green or how much yellow you want to put in the page. You can make a color dark or light by setting RGB values. Another popular method is setting the HEX codes. Different colors have been allocated six-digit codes that represent the amount of red, blue, and green or any other color. These codes start with a # sign, followed by a combination of alphabets and numbers.

Text Colors

You can use names of colors as you have seen how I used them on different web pages. There are a total of 147 predefined color names that are easily recognizable by web browsers. If you use one of them, you don't have to fill in the codes. There is also another way to specify colors in CSS, which is known as HSLA.

By using CSS comments, you can remember which color is going to apply on a certain piece of text. You will not have to juggle between the browser and code editor to confirm. Add a comment with each color code. I will be applying different methods to apply colors on the webpage. (Duckett, 2011)

```
<html>

<body>

<h1 style="color:Tomato;">Let me tell you a
story.</h1>

<h2 style="color:Navy;">The story is a short
one.</h2>

<p style="color: Pink;"> Once, there was an
eagle that flew high in the skies,

<br> touching upon the tip of the mountains.

<br> One day she found a ring, stuck in the
branch of an apple tree.</p>

<p style="color:Orange;">She took it and flew to
her nest. While playing with it, she got her
head stuck in it.
```

```
<br>She didn't panic or hit her head on the
stump of a tree to get rid of it.
<br>One day she drenched her head in oil and the
ring came off of her neck.</p>
</body>
</html>
```

Let's see which colors we get from the above code example.

Let me tell you a story.

The story is a short one.

Once, there was an eagle that flew high in the skies,
touching upon the tip of the mountains.
One day she found a ring stuck in the branch of an apple tree.

She took it and flew to her nest. While playing with it, she got her head stuck in it.

She didn't panic or hit her head on the stump of a tree to get rid of it.

Then, one day she drenched her head in oil and the ring came off of her neck.

You can add background to all paragraphs separately to make them more lively, interactive and appealing to the visitors of your webpage. Lets' see how to do that.

```
<html>
<body>
```

```
<h1 style="background-color:Tomato;">Let me tell
you a story.</h1>

<h2 style="background-color:Navy;">The story is
a short one.</h2>

<p style="background-color:Pink;"> Once, there
was an eagle that flew high in the skies,

<br> touching upon the tip of the mountains.

<br> One day she found a ring, stuck in the
branch of an apple tree. </p>

<p style="background-color:Orange;"> She took it
and flew to her nest. While playing with it, she
got her head stuck in it.

<br>She didn't panic or hit her head on the
stump of a tree to get rid of it.

<br>One day she drenched her head in oil and the
ring came off of her neck.</p>

</body>

</html>
```

The display of the rule can be seen as under:

Let me tell you a story.

The story is a short one.

Once, there was an eagle that flew high in the skies,
touching upon the tip of the mountains.
One day she found a ring stuck in the branch of an apple tree.

She took it and flew to her nest. While playing with it, she got her
head stuck in it.

She didn't panic or hit her head on the stump of the tree to get rid of it.

One day she drenched her head in oil and the ring came off of her neck.

We have already discussed how to change the colors of the border simply by defining the name of the color. You can refer back to the past chapters to skim through the same. Now, that's the easy part. I will be now be moving on to other complicated but efficient methods of filling colors on your web page. The first option to consider is CSS RGB Value.

CSS RGB Value

We can specify a color in CSS through RGB values. The formula is rgb (red, green, blue). Here each parameter such as red, green and blue tends to define how intense color should be. The intensity can be set from 0 to 255. For example, if you display rgb(0,255,0), the color your visitors will see will be green because you have set it to the maximum value. The others are set at zero. If you want to display the black color, you have to set all the parameters to zero. If you want to display white, you have to raise the parameters to the maximum value that is 255. Let's try it out in the editor.

```
<html>

<body>

<h1 style="background-color:rgb(255,0,0);">Let
me tell you a story about an eagle.</h1>
```

```
<h2 style="background-
color:rgb(111,220,55);">This is a short
story.</h2>

<p style="background-color:rgb(0,0,100);"> Once,
there was an eagle that flew high in the skies,

<br> touching upon the tip of the mountains.

<br> One day she found a ring, stuck in the
branch of an apple tree.</p>

<p style="background-color:rgb(195,50,200);">She
took it and flew to her nest. While playing with
it, she got her head stuck in it.

<br>She didn't panic or hit her head on the
stump of a tree to get rid of it.

<br>One day she drenched her head in oil and the
ring came off of her neck.</p>

</body>

</html>
```

RGB can be an exciting thing to use on your webpages. RGB coloring system is usually found in a wide range of design applications, as well as other technologies. For the past few years, it has become prevalent among web designers. They are relishing the fruits RGB has brought to them. You can use RGB colors by putting the values inside parenthesis. Let's change the values and see how they affect the colors.

```
<html>

<body>

<h1 style="background-
color:rgb(100,150,200);">Let me tell you a story
of an eagle.</h1>
```

```
<h2 style="background-
color:rgb(11,20,155);">This is a short
story.</h2>

<p style="background-color:rgb(60,80,200);">
Once, there was an eagle that flew high in the
skies,

<br> touching upon the tip of the mountains.

<br> One day she found a ring, stuck in the
branch of an apple tree.</p>

<p style="background-color:rgb(50,220,100);">
She took it and flew to her nest. While playing
with it, she got her head stuck in it.

<br>She didn't panic or hit her head on the
stump of a tree to get rid of it.

<br>One day she drenched her head in oil and the
ring came off of her neck.</p>

</body>

</html>
```

(CSS Colors, n.d)

The RGB property offers an interesting opportunity to apply gray shading to your web pages. You can go for pitch black, dark gray, light gray, and even the lightest gray color schemes. Let's change the values of RGB property to have the desired results.

```
<html>

<body>

<h1 style="background-
color:rgb(255,255,255);">Let me tell you a story
of an eagle.</h1>
```

```
<h2 style="background-
color:rgb(100,100,100);">This is a short
story.</h2>

<p style="background-color:rgb(0,0,0);"> Once,
there was an eagle that flew high in the skies,

<br> touching upon the tip of the mountains.

<br> One day she found a ring, stuck in the
branch of an apple tree.</p>

<p style="background-color:rgb(150,150,150);">
She took it and flew to her nest. While playing
with it, she got her head stuck in it.

<br>She didn't panic or hit her head on the
stump of a tree to get rid of it.

<br>One day she drenched her head in oil and the
ring came off of her neck.</p>

</body>

</html>
```

If you run the code, you will have a variety of gray shading on the webpage. If you keep changing the RGB value, you will be able to get different shades. Try it by changing the value.

(CSS Colors, n.d)

You might have noticed by now that each color is applied to a piece of text in the form of a box. Why not in circles? Its reason is that CSS takes each HTML element as enclosed inside a box; that's why the background property sets the color for that box. By default, the color is white, as you have seen in different examples. You don't have to specify white in CSS property.

One of the major benefits of practicing RGB in the CSS style code is the power you get to control how opaque your color should look. You can add an 'a' to the rgb (), which enables you to include a fourth value. This additional value will determine the level of transparency on a scale from zero to one.

```
<html>

<body>

<h1 style="background-
color:rgb(255,255,255);">Let me tell you a story
of an eagle.</h1>

<h2 style="background-color:rgb(150,150,150,
0.2);">This is a short story.</h2>

<p style="background-color:rgb(150,150,150,
1);"> Once, there was an eagle that flew high in
the skies,

<br> touching upon the tip of the mountains.

<br> One day she found a ring, stuck in the
branch of an apple tree.</p>

<p style="background-color:rgb(150,150,150,
0.5);"> She took it and flew to her nest. While
playing with it, she got her head stuck in it.

<br>She didn't panic or hit her head on the
stump of a tree to get rid of it.

<br>One day she drenched her head in oil and the
ring came off of her neck.</p>

</body>

</html>
```

I have set the rgb value for three different html elements at the same but changed the fourth value. It is going to greatly affect the transparency of the background color. You can see the effects by running the code.

CSS HEX Value

There is another method of applying colors on your web pages. You will have to put in a color code, which generally is a sort of hexadecimal value. Some of the hexadecimal values include rr(red), bb(blue) as well as gg(green). The code is #rrggbb. In the hexadecimal values, the range starts from 00 and ends up at 255. Let's create a code.

```
#ff0000
```

Now we have set the red color to the full while set the other two colors at zero to the lowest value. HEX codes are considered as the most common technique for adding colors to html elements. Also, HEX codes allow you to change and set the default color of the text of your website.

```
<html>
<body>
<h1 style="background-color:#00ff00;">Let me
tell you a story.</h1>
<h2 style="background-color:#0000ff;">The story
is a short one.</h2>
<p style="background-color:#2cb277;"> Once,
there was an eagle that flew high in the skies,
<br> touching upon the tip of the mountains.
<br> One day she found a ring, stuck in the
branch of an apple tree. </p>
```

```
<p style="background-color:5a4abc;"> She took it
and flew to her nest. While playing with it, she
got her head stuck in it.

<br>She didn't panic or hit her head on the
stump of a tree to get rid of it.

<br>One day she drenched her head in oil and the
ring came off of her neck.</p>

</body>

</html>
```

Like the previous method, this one too offers gray shading. As you have learned that there are three pairs in the code, you can fill in the page with gray colors by using equal values for three light sources. Let's demonstrate it in the code editor.

```
<html>

<body>

<h1 style="background-color:#434343;">Let me
tell you a story.</h1>

<h2 style="background-color:#bcbcbc;">The story
is a short one.</h2>

<p style="background-color:#asasas;"> Once,
there was an eagle that flew high in the skies,

<br> touching upon the tip of the mountains.

<br> One day she found a ring, stuck in the
branch of an apple tree.</p>

<p style="background-color:#989898;">She took it
and flew to her nest. While playing with it, she
got her head stuck in it.

<br>She didn't panic or hit her head on the
stump of a tree to get rid of it.
```

93

```
<br>One day she drenched her head in oil and the
ring came off of her neck.</p>
</body>
</html>
```

We have the display in black and gray. Let's see how it looks.

Let me tell you a story.

The story is a short one.

Once, there was an eagle that flew high in the skies,
touching upon the tip of the mountains.
One day she found a ring stuck in the branch of an apple tree.

She took it and flew to her nest. While playing with it, she got her
head stuck in it.
She didn't panic and hit her head on the stump of the tree to get rid
of it.
One day she drenched her head in oil and the ring came off of her
neck.

HSL Value

CSS offers great diversity when it comes to applying colors to a webpage. You can specify colors with the help of h for hues, s for saturation, and l for lightness. Hue can be adjusted from 0 to 360. In this 360-point wheel, 0 denotes red, 120 denoted green, and 240 indicate blue. The second alphabet S is applied as a percentage value in which 0% denotes gray while 100 % denotes full color. The third alphabet L indicates percentage in which 0 represents black, 50, is in between light and dark while 100% is full white.

Basically, HSL stands for Hue, Saturation and Lightness. This adds more to the already diverse color system in CSS language.

```
<html>

<body>

<h1 style="background-
color:hsl(0,100%,50%);">Let me tell you a
story.</h1>

<h2 style="background-
color:hsl(200,100%,50%);">The story is a short
one.</h2>

<p style="background-color:hsl(39,22%,70%);">
Once, there was an eagle that flew high in the
skies,

<br> touching upon the tip of the mountains.

<br> One day she found a ring, stuck in the
branch of an apple tree. </p>

<p style="background-
color:hsl(300,55%,60%);">She took it and flew to
her nest. While playing with it, she got her
head stuck in it.

<br>She didn't panic or hit her head on the
stump of a tree to get rid of it.

<br>One day she drenched her head in oil and the
ring came off of her neck.</p>

</body>

</html>
```

(CSS Colors, n.d)

If you carefully read the above code, you can see that in the middle comes saturation. I set saturation percentage at 100% for the h1 and h2. For paragraphs, I lowered the level. If you want pure color, you should set it to 100%. At 50% it will have 50% element of gray but the color will dominate the background. At 0%, you will see only gray. There will be no color at all.

```
<html>

<body>

<h1 style="background-color:hsl(0,0%,50%);">Let
me tell you a story of an eagle.</h1>

<h2 style="background-
color:hsl(200,0%,50%);">This is a short
story.</h2>

<p style="background-color:hsl(39,0%,70%);">
Once, there was an eagle that flew high in the
skies,

<br> touching upon the tip of the mountains.

<br> One day she found a ring, stuck in the
branch of an apple tree. </p>

<p style="background-color:hsl(300,0%,60%);">She
took it and flew to her nest. While playing with
it, she got her head stuck in it.

<br>She didn't panic or hit her head on the
stump of a tree to get rid of it.

<br>One day she drenched her head in oil and the
ring came off of her neck.</p>

</body>

</html>
```

You can also set the lightness in the third category. Lightness of a color is described as the amount of light that you need to apply on the color you have selected. If you keep it at 0%, there will be no light. At 50%, the light factor will be 50%, and if you set it to 100%, it means you have set it to full light.

The Alpha Factor

RGBA contains an additional alpha factor in combination with rgb. This factor decides how opaque or transparent your colors will appear. Let's see the pattern.

rgba(red, green, blue, alpha)

The alpha parameter ranges from 0.0 to 1.0. The alpha factor is also an extension of HSL color values. There too it has the same job as in rgb property. Let's see the property.

hsla(hue, saturation, lightness, alpha)

The range 0.0 denotes a fully transparent result while 1.0 denotes no transparency at all.

```
<html>
<body>
<h1 style="background-
color:rgba(255,99,71,0);">Let me tell you a
story.</h1>
<h2 style="background-
color:rgba(255,99,71,1);">The story is a short
one.</h2>
```

```
<p style="background-color:hsl(39,50%,70%,
0.5);"> Once, there was an eagle that flew high
in the skies,

<br> touching upon the tip of the mountains.

<br> One day she found a ring, stuck in the
branch of an apple tree.</p>

<p style="background-color:hsl(300,100%,60%,
0.8);"> She took it and flew to her nest. While
playing with it, she got her head stuck in it.

<br>She didn't panic or hit her head on the
stump of a tree to get rid of it.

<br>One day she drenched her head in oil and the
ring came off of her neck.</p>

</body>

</html>
```

Chapter 7

CSS Outline, Boxes

CSS is like an ornament for an HTML document. If you master the art of applying CSS rules, you can be a fantastic web designer because you will have so many options at hand to beautify your web page. You can give style to each element and customize its appearance so that the webpage could suit the taste of your visitors.

With the help of CSS outline property; you can enclose HTML elements inside it. We have already covered the subject of borders. In this chapter, we will see how we can place outlines around pieces of text. After that, we will move on to CSS boxes.

You can do lots of things with CSS boxes like setting its dimensions, putting them in borders, setting margins, and also padding for the boxes.

CSS Outline

An outline is usually drawn around HTML elements just outside the borders if you want that element to stand out among the rest of the elements on a page. There are some properties for the creation of outlines. These features include outline-style, outline-color, outline-offset, and out-line width. Outline is different from borders. It may overlap with other content. Also, it is not a part of the dimensions of an element. Let's test different types of outline styles in the code editor.

```
<html>
<body>
<head>
<style>
h1 {outline-color:violet;}
h2 {outline-color:red;}
p {outline-color:pink;}
h1.solid {outline-style:solid;}
h2.dotted {outline-style:dotted;}
p.dotted {outline-style: dotted;}
p.ridge {outline-style: ridge;}
p.outset {outline-style: outset;}
p.inset {outline-style: inset;}
p.groove {outline-style: groove;}
p.solid {outline-style: solid;}
p.dashed {outline-style: dashed;}
p.double {outline-style: double;}
</style>
</head>
<body>
<h1 class="solid">Let me tell you a story of an
eagle.</h1>
<h2 class="dotted">This is a short story.</h2>
<p class="dotted">Once, there was an eagle that
flew high in the skies.</p>
```

```
<p class="ridge">She touched upon the tips of
the mountains.</p>

<p class="outset">She wanted to fly higher above
the clouds.</p>

<p class="inset">One day she found a ring stuck
in a branch of an apple tree.</p>

<p class="groove">She took it and flew to her
nest.</p>

<p class="solid">She had no use of the ring.</p>

<p class="dashed">Still she desired to use
it.</p>

<p class="double">She got her head stuck in it
while playing with it.</p>

</body>

</html>
```

In the next HTML document, I will add color to each outline and set its width. Learning about outlines help a lot in tasks that involve posting important announcements on the website. For example, you are about to run a sales campaign on your website. To market the campaign, you can put the announcement in an outline to engage more visitors toward it. Add the colors of your choice and make it feel its presence on the page. I'll be adding the color factor and the width factor in the same HTML document below. Let's see how to do that.

```
<html>

<body>

<head>

<style>
```

```
h1.solid {
    border: 3px green;
    outline-style:solid;
    outline-color:black
    outline width:thick;
    }

h2.dotted {
    border: 2px violet;
    outline-style:dotted;
    outline-color:violet;
    outline width:thin;
    }
p.dashed {
    border: 3px red;
    outline-style: dashed;
    outline-color:green;
    outline width:4px;
    }
p.ridge {outline-style: ridge;}
p.outset {outline-style: outset;}
p.inset {outline-style: inset;}
p.groove {outline-style: groove;}
p.double {outline-style: double;}
</style>
</head>
```

```
<body>

<h1 class="solid">Let me tell you a story of an
eagle.</h1>

<h2 class="dotted">This is a short story.</h2>

<p class="dotted">Once, there was an eagle that
flew high in the skies.</p>

<p class="ridge">She touched upon the tips of
the mountains.</p>

<p class="outset">She wanted to fly higher above
the clouds.</p>

<p class="inset">One day she found a ring stuck
in a branch of an apple tree.</p>

<p class="groove">She took it and flew to her
nest.</p>

<p class="solid">She had no use of the ring.</p>

<p class="dashed">Still she desired to use
it.</p>

<p class="double">She got her head into it while
playing with it.</p>

</body>

</html>
```

(CSS Outline, n.d)

CSS Box

Usually every HTML element is placed inside a box although the box remains invisible. A CSS box is by default big enough to hold all the contents. You can customize the box by adjusting the dimensions for the box. You can add the height as well as width properties. You can use pixels, percentages as well as ems to specify the size of the box. However, pixels top all the three methods because of its popularity among web designers. Pixels help you create a box that has particular size that is relevant to browser's size. If a box is contained in another box, the percentage of the size will be of the containing box.

A CSS box consists of margins, borders, and padding. One thing I missed is content that can be a piece of text or an image. Padding is the clear area that is around the content. In most cases, padding remains transparent. Then comes the border that covers the padding as well as the content. Margin encloses upon the border. This, like padding, is transparent.

```
<html>
<head>
<style>
div {
    background-color: pink;
    width: 200px;
    border: 25px solid blue;
    padding: 100px;
    margin: 30px;
}
</style>
</head>
<body>
<h1> Let me narrate a short story.</h1>
<p> Once, there was an eagle that flew high in
the skies,
```

```
<br> touching upon the tip of the mountains.

<br> One day she found a ring, stuck in the
branch of an apple tree.</p>

<div>She took it and flew to her nest. While
playing with it, she got her head stuck in it.

<br>She didn't panic or hit her head on the
stump of a tree to get rid of it.

<br>One day she drenched her head in oil and the
ring came off of her neck.</div>

</body>

</html>
```

If you run the code in the browser, you will see a box enclosing the piece of text which is inside the div brackets. Let's change the values in CSS properties and see the result.

```
<html>

<head>

<style>

div {

    background-color: azure;

    width: 700px;

    border: 30px solid violet;

    padding: 50px;

    margin: 20px;

}

</style>

</head>

<body>
```

```html
<h1> Let me narrate a story.</h1>
<p> Once, there was an eagle that flew high in
the skies,
<br> touching upon the tip of the mountains.
<br> One day she found a ring, stuck in the
branch of an apple tree.</p>
<div>She took it and flew to her nest. While
playing with it, she got her head stuck in it.
<br>She didn't panic or hit her head on the
stump of a tree to get rid of it.
<br>One day she drenched her head in oil and the
ring came off of her neck.</div>
</body>
</html>
```

In this example, you can see that the box is in horizontal shape. This happened because I changed the value of width of the box. You can experiment some other values for the width property and see different results. Boxes are a necessity for a web page because you need them to display an important announcement or some other key piece of information about your products or services such as a sales message.

Chapter 8

CSS Links, Tables, and Forms

There are many CSS properties that you can use to work with links and tables. This chapter is going to walk you through the process of styling CSS links, tables, and forms to make them reader-friendly and beautiful. You will learn how you can add color to each column of the table to make it stands out of the rest. Similarly, you will also learn how to beautify the forms such as submissions forms, survey forms and any other form that you have created in HTML.

You will be able to create beautiful buttons that can be integrated into the forms. The chapter contains a wide range of code examples that would touch upon all the topics. Each code example also contains the displayed results of the code. You can take up the code, recreate it, modify or run it to see how it works. Even simply reading it will give you a general idea of how you have to proceed.

```html
<html>
<head>
<style>
a {
    color: green;
}
}
</style>
```

```
</head>
<body>
<h1> Let me tell you a story.</h1>
<h2><b><a href="default.asp"
target="_blank">Watch the video story
here.</a></b></h2>
<p> Once, there was an eagle that flew high in
the skies,
<br> touching upon the tip of the mountains.
<br> One day she found a ring, stuck in the
branch of an apple tree. </p>
<p>She took it and flew to her nest. While
playing with it, she got her head stuck in it.
<br>She didn't panic or hit her head on the
stump of a tree to get rid of it.
<br>One day she drenched her head in oil and the
ring came off of her neck.</p>
</body>
</html>
```

The result of the above style is as under. You can see the second line of code which has got a link hidden inside.

Let me tell you a story.

<u>Watch the video story here.</u>

Once, there was an eagle that flew high in the skies,
touching upon the tip of the mountains.
One day she found a ring stuck in the branch of an apple tree.

108

She took it and flew to her nest. While playing with it, she got her head stuck in it.

She didn't panic or hit her head on the stump of a tree to get rid of it.

Then, one day she drenched her head in oil and the ring came off of her neck.

CSS links are critical because many a time you have to connect your webpage to another website to offer your users an amazing and fruitful experience. There are four kinds of links that you can use for different purposes. They are named as a: link, a: hover, a: active, a: visited. Each link has a specific purpose. For example, a: hover is used to allow users to hover over the mouse on the link and make it open. Let's try to create links by all the four methods.

```html
<html>
<head>
<style>
/* This is an unvisited link */
a:link {
    color: green;
}
/* This is a visited link. */
a:visited {
    color: blue;
}
/* This is a hover link. */
```

```css
a:hover {

    color: violet;

}

/* This is a selected link. */

a:active {

    color: red;

}
```
```html
</style>

</head>

<body>

<h1> Let me tell you a story.</h1>

<h2><b><a href="default.asp"
target="_blank">Watch the video story
here.</a></b></h2>

<p> Once, there was an eagle that flew high in
the skies,

<br> touching upon the tip of the mountains.

<br> One day she found a ring, stuck in the
branch of an apple tree.</p>

<p>She took it and flew to her nest. While
playing with it, she got her head stuck in it.

<br>She didn't panic or hit her head on the
stump of a tree to get rid of it.

<br>One day she drenched her head in oil and the
ring came off of her neck.</p>

</body>

</html>
```

You might be thinking that I had entered four links, but just one color can be seen in the results if you have already tested the code. Links change their status. In the start, they are unvisited. Then you hover your mouse over them. Then you click them open and leave them visited. So, technically, you can add four different colors according to the status of your link. Let's see what else we can do with the links. Also, we can decorate the text of links and also add color to the background. Let's see how to do that.

```html
<html>
<head>
<style>
/* This is an unvisited link */
a:link {
    color: green;
    text-decoration: none;
    background-color: yellow
}
/* This is a visited link. */
a:visited {
    color: blue;
    text-decoration: none;
    background-color: gray
}
/* This is a hover link. */
a:hover {
    color: violet;
    text-decoration: underline;
    background-color: pink
}
```

```
/* This is a selected link. */
a:active {
    color: red;
    text-decoration: underline;
    background-color: hotpink
}
</style>
</head>
<body>
<h1> Let me tell you a story.</h1>
<h2><b><a href="default.asp"
target="_blank">Watch the video story
here.</a></b></h2>
<p> Once, there was an eagle that flew high in
the skies,
<br> touching upon the tip of the mountains.
<br> One day she found a ring, stuck in the
branch of an apple tree.</p>
<p>  She took it and flew to her nest. While
playing with it, she got her head stuck into it.
<br> She didn't panic and hit her head into the
stump of the tree to get rid of it.
<br> One day she drenched her head in oil and
the ring moved out of her neck. </p>
</body>
</html>
```

(CSS Links, n.d)

CSS Tables

CSS allows you to transform the way your tables look in HTML. You can add colors to the headings and to the columns. You can change the font style and font size of the text inside the tables. Let's create one.

```
<!DOCTYPE html>
<html>
<head>
<style>
#countries {
   font-family: "Courier New", Gerogia,
Helvetica, sans-serif;
   border-collapse: collapse;
   width: 80%;
}
#countries td, #countries th {
   border: 2px solid green;
   padding: 6px;
}
#countries tr:nth-child(even){background-color:
violet;}
#countries tr:hover {background-color: #ddd;}
#countries th {
   padding-top: 15px;
   padding-bottom: 15px;
   text-align: left;
```

```
      background-color: #ffAc2b;
      color: gray;
  }
</style>
</head>
<body>
<table id="countries">
  <tr>
    <th>Country</th>
    <th>Capital</th>
    <th>Reasons for fame</th>
  </tr>
  <tr>
    <td>Germany</td>
    <td>Berlin</td>
    <td>BMW</td>
  </tr>
  <tr>
    <td>United States of America</td>
    <td>Washington DC</td>
    <td>Marvel</td>
  </tr>
  <tr>
    <td>China</td>
    <td>Beijing</td>
    <td>cheap products</td>
```

```
</tr>
<tr>
  <td>Pakistan</td>
  <td>Islamabad</td>
  <td>Footballs</td>
</tr>
<tr>
  <td>Japan</td>
  <td>Tokyo</td>
  <td>Robotics</td>
</tr>
<tr>
  <td>United Kingdom</td>
  <td>London</td>
  <td>Thames</td>
</tr>
<tr>
  <td>Egypt</td>
  <td>Cairo</td>
  <td>Pyramids</td>
</tr>
<tr>
  <td>India</td>
  <td>New Delhi</td>
  <td>Taj Mehal</td>
</tr>
```

```
<tr>
    <td>Brazil</td>
    <td>Sao Paulo</td>
    <td>Statue of Jesus</td>
</tr>
<tr>
    <td>Kingdom of Saudi Arabia</td>
    <td>Riyadh</td>
    <td>Pilgrimage</td>
</tr>
</table>
</body>
</html>
```

The results of the above code example can be seen below. You can change the values and yield out a different output in the internet browser. Tables are an essential element for a web page. You need them if you are running a website that displays information about the rise and fall in the prices of stock market shares. If you don't style them properly with CSS, your visitors are not going to like their dull and boring look. Appropriately colored tables appear well on the website and keep visitors engaged for a while.

Country	Capital	Reasons for fame
Germany	Berlin	BMW
United States of America	Washington DC	Marvel
China	Beijing	cheap products
Pakistan	Islamabad	Footballs
Japan	Tokyo	Robotics
United Kingdom	London	Thames
Egypt	Cairo	Pyramids
India	New Delhi	Taj Mehal
Brazil	Sao Paulo	Statue of Jesus
Kingdom of Saudi Arabia	Riyadh	Pilgrimage

You can alter the colors, the border, and padding by making slight changes in the HTML document. You can also add more columns and rows to suit your specific requirement. In the above example, I have added background colors, padding, border colors and have also adjusted the width of the columns. You can take the example document and customize for learning practice. (CSS Tables, n.d).

CSS Forms

HTML provides us with an easy way to create different types of forms that we can use to collect user information like their usernames, passwords, and email addresses. Some are subscription forms while others are survey forms. When we create an HTML form, its look is rigid and dull. Thanks to CSS, we can change that. We can make it look exceptionally well. Let's create a form and then transform its look by adding some simple CSS properties.

```
<!DOCTYPE html>
<html>
<style>
input[type=text], select {
    width: 100%;
    padding: 15px 25px;
    margin: 10px 0;
    display: inline-block;
    border: 2px solid green;
    border-radius: 6px;
    box-sizing: border-box;
}
input[type=submit] {
    width: 50%;
    background-color: pink;
    color: black;
    padding: 12px 18px;
    margin: 10px 0;
```

```css
  border: 2px solid green;

  border-radius: 2px;

  cursor: pointer;

  font-size: 25px

}

input[type=submit]:hover {

  background-color: #45b049;

}

div {

  border-radius: 4px;

  background-color: #f1f1f1;

  padding: 15px;

}

</style>

<body>

<h1>I will be using CSS to style this raw HTML
Form</h1>

<div>

  <form action="/action_page.php">

    <label for="name">Please enter your first
Name</label>

    <input type="text" id="name"
name="firstname" placeholder="Plese enter
here..">

    <label for="lname">Please enter your last
Name</label>

    <input type="text" id="lname"
name="lastname" placeholder="Please enter
here..">
```

```
    <label for="country">Where do you
live?</label>
    <select id="country" name="country">
      <option value="USA">USA</option>
      <option value="canada">Canada</option>
      <option value="UK">UK</option>
      <option value="china">China</option>
      <option value="pakistan">Pakistan</option>
      <option value="france">France</option>
    </select>

    <input type="submit" value="Submit">
  </form>
 </div>
 </body>
 </html>
```

The result is as under:

I have styled the border, the input fields, the submit button and a lot more. Let's learn more about styling the buttons, as they are an important part of forms on your web page.

```
<!DOCTYPE html>
<html>
<head>
<style>
input[type=refresh], input[type=submit],
input[type=process] {
  background-color: #4CAFBB;
  border: 2px solid green;
  color: white;
  padding: 19px 34px;
  text-decoration: none;
  margin: 6px 4px;
  cursor: pointer;
}
</style>
</head>
<body>
<h1>You are seeing styled input buttons.</h1>
<input type="refresh" value="Refresh It">
<input type="process" value="Process">
<input type="submit" value="Submit">
</body>
</html>
```

The result is as under:

In the end let's see an example of a complete form.

```
<!DOCTYPE html>
<html>
<head>
<style>
* {
  box-sizing: border-box;
}
input[type=text], select, textarea {
  width: 50%;
  padding: 8px;
  border: 1px solid #bbb;
  border-radius: 2px;
  resize: vertical;
}
label {
  padding: 10px 10px 10px 0;
  display: inline-block;
}
input[type=submit] {
  background-color: #4CAF50;
```

```css
  color: white;
  padding: 10px 18px;
  border: none;
  border-radius: 4px;
  cursor: pointer;
  float: right;
}
input[type=submit]:hover {
  background-color: #45a049;
}
.container {
  border-radius: 7px;
  background-color: #f2f2f2;
  padding: 15px;
}
.col-25 {
  float: left;
  width: 50%;
  margin-top: 4px;
}
.col-75 {
  float: left;
  width: 50%;
  margin-top: 4px;
}
/* Clear floats */
```

```
.row:after {

  content: "";

  display: table;

  clear: both;

}

/* Responsive layout  */

@media screen and (max-width: 400px) {

  .col-25, .col-75, input[type=submit] {

    width: 50%;

    margin-top: 0;

  }

}

</style>

</head>

<body>

<h2>This is an example of a responsive Form</h2>

<p>You will have to resize the browser window to
see the effect.</p>

<div class="container">

  <form action="/action_page.php">

  <div class="row">

    <div class="col-25">

      <label for="nname">Please enter your First
Name</label>

    </div>

    <div class="col-75">
```

```html
        <input type="text" id="fname"
name="firstname" placeholder="Please enter
here..">

    </div>

  </div>

  <div class="row">

    <div class="col-25">

      <label for="lname">Please enter your Last
Name</label>

    </div>

    <div class="col-75">

      <input type="text" id="lname"
name="lastname" placeholder="Please enter
here..">

    </div>

  </div>

  <div class="row">

    <div class="col-25">

      <label for="country">Please choose your
country</label>

    </div>

    <div class="col-75">

      <select id="country" name="country">

        <option value="usa">USA</option>

        <option value="canada">Canada</option>

        <option value="uk">UK</option>

      </select>

    </div>
```

```
    </div>

    <div class="row">

      <div class="col-25">

        <label for="bio">Please enter your bio
here.</label>

      </div>

      <div class="col-75">

        <textarea id="bio" name="bio"
placeholder="Write here.."
style="height:200px"></textarea>

      </div>

    </div>

    <div class="row">

      <input type="submit" value="Submit">

    </div>

    </form>

  </div>

  </body>

  </html>
```

Your form will look like this:

(CSS Forms, n.d)

Chapter 9

CSS Images and Lists

You can control the size of images on a webpage and also align them by using CSS rules that would affect the presentation of the page. CSS allows you to achieve several interesting effects by integrating background images on your webpage. You can specify the size as well as the alignment of the image you have to use. This chapter will walk you through the process of adding images to different boxes in CSS and also creating image rollovers.

First, take a look at controlling the size of the CSS images with the help of height and width properties in CSS. When you have specified the size of an image, it will be easier for the web page to load in the browser, because CSS code will tell the browser how much space is to be left for each image? In this way, your webpage will smoothly load in the browser.

Many websites use same-sized images on different web pages rather than specifying the size of the image for each page. Take the example of any online selling shop. Each product listing has the same sized images of different products. You will be using <img> element in the HTML. You will have to add selectors for class names, and after that, you will have to include width and height attributes for controlling the dimensions of the image. Let's see how to integrate an image inside the HTML code.

```
<html>
<head>
<style>
img {
    border-radius: 10px;
}
</style>
</head>
<body>
<h1> Let me tell you a story.</h1>
<h2>The story is about an eagle.</h2>
<img src="eagle.jpg" alt="Eagle" width="300"
height="200">
<p> Once, there was an eagle that flew high in
the skies,
<br> touching upon the tip of the mountains.
<br> One day she found a ring, stuck in the
branch of an apple tree.</p>
<p>She took it and flew to her nest. While
playing with it, she got her head stuck in it.
<br>She didn't panic or hit her head on the
stump of a tree to get rid of it.
<br>One day she drenched her head in oil and the
ring came off of her neck.</p>
</body>
</html>
```

The image will appear as under on the Internet browser.

Let me tell you a story.

The story is about an eagle.

Once, there was an eagle that flew high in the skies, touching upon the tip of the mountains.
One day she found a ring stuck in the branch of an apple tree.

She took it and flew to her nest. While playing with it, she got her head stuck in it.
She didn't panic or hit her head on the stump of the tree to get rid of it.
One day she drenched her head in oil and the ring came off of her neck.

Rounded Images

We also have the option of adding an image to the CSS sheet in a rounded form. That's quite an interesting feature. Round images not only look better than square images, but they become a necessity sometimes. Let's try how we can add images on a CSS sheet in a rounded shape. All you have to do is to adjust the height and weight of the image in perfect balance.

```
<html>
<head>
<style>
img {
    border-radius: 50%;
}
</style>
</head>
<body>
<h1> Let me tell you a story.</h1>
<h2>The story is about an eagle.</h2>
<img src="eagle.jpg" alt="Eagle" width="400"
height="400">
<p> Once, there was an eagle that flew high in
the skies,
<br> touching upon the tip of the mountains.
<br> One day she found a ring, stuck in the
branch of an apple tree.</p>
<p>She took it and flew to her nest. While
playing with it, she got her head stuck in it.
<br>She didn't panic or hit her head on the
stump of a tree
to get rid of it.
<br>One day she drenched her head in oil and the
ring came
```

```
off of her neck.</p>
</body>
</html>
```

There are plenty of options that you can use to place images. I will be adding images now in the start of the paragraph as well as in the middle of the paragraph.

```
<html>
<head>
<style>
img {
    border-radius: 10px;
}
</style>
</head>
<body>
<h1> Let me tell you a story.</h1>
<h2>The story is about an eagle.</h2>
<p> Once, there was an eagle that flew high in
the skies,
<br> touching upon the tip of the mountains.
<br> One day she found a ring, stuck in the
branch of an apple tree.</p>
<p><img src="eagle.jpg" alt="Eagle"
width="300">She took it and flew to her nest.
While playing with it, she got her head stuck in
it.
<br>She didn't panic or hit her head on the
stump of a tree
```

to get rid of it.

One day she drenched her head in oil and the ring came

off of her neck.</p>

</body>

</html>

In the next example, I'll be inserting the image in between the piece of text. Let's see how to do that.

<html>

<head>

<style>

img {

    border-radius: 10px;

}

</style>

</head>

<body>

<h1> Let me tell you a story.</h1>

<h2>The story is about an eagle.</h2>

<p>Once, there was an eagle that flew high in the skies.
She touched the tip of the mountains.
 One day she found a ring stuck in a branch of an apple tree.
 She took it and flew to her nest.<img src="eagle.jpg" alt="Eagle" width="100" height="100"> As a result, she got her head stick in it while playing with it.
 She embraced it as a mark of distinction among fellow eagles.
 One day

she drenched her head in oil and the ring came off of her neck.</p>

</body>

</html>

Let's create thumbnail images by using the border property of CSS. Let's move on to the editor.

```
<html>

<head>

<style>

img {

    border: 2px solid #ccc

    border-radius: 10px;

    padding: 10px;

    width: 100px;

}

</style>

</head>

<body>

<h1> Let me tell you a story.</h1>

<h2>The story is about an eagle.</h2>

<img src="eagle.jpg" alt="Eagle"
style="width:150px">

<p> Once, there was an eagle that flew high in
the skies,

<br> touching upon the tip of the mountains.

<br> One day she found a ring, stuck in the
branch of an apple tree.
```

```
<br> She took it and flew to her nest. While
playing with it, she got her head stuck in it.

<br> She didn't panic or hit her head on the
stump of a tree to get rid of it.

<br> Instead, she embraced it as a mark of
distinction among fellow eagles.

<br> Then, one day she drenched her head in oil
and the ring came off of her neck.</p>

</body>

</html>
```

You cannot expect your visitors to use just a personal computer to visit your website. She can use a mobile phone and a tablet as well. That's why your website should be responsive to any device your visitor is using. Otherwise, you are likely to lose customers. Let's try to create some responsive images.

```
<html>

<head>

<style>

img {

    max-width: 100%;

    height: auto;

}

</style>

</head>

<body>

<h1> Let me tell you a story.</h1>

<h2>The story is about an eagle.</h2>
```

```
<img src="eagle.jpg" alt="Eagle" width="500"
height="200">

<p> Once, there was an eagle that flew high in
the skies,

<br> touching upon the tip of the mountains.

<br> One day she found a ring, stuck in the
branch of an apple tree.

<br> She took it and flew to her nest. While
playing with it, she got her head stuck in it.

<br> She didn't panic or hit her head on the
stump of a tree to get rid of it.

<br> Instead, she embraced it as a mark of
distinction among fellow eagles.

<br> Then, one day she drenched her head in oil
and the ring came off of her neck.</p>

</body>

</html>
```

(CSS Styling Images, n.d)

Centralizing an Image

I will be centralizing the image in the code example that is given below.

```
<html>

<head>

<style>

img {

    display: block;

    margin-right: auto;
```

```
      margin-left: auto;
  }
</style>
</head>
<body>
<h1> Let me tell you a story.</h1>
<h2>The story is about an eagle.</h2>
<img src="eagle.jpg" alt="Eagle"
style="width:30%">
<p> Once, there was an eagle that flew high in
the skies,
<br> touching upon the tip of the mountains.
<br> One day she found a ring, stuck in the
branch of an apple tree.
<br> She took it and flew to her nest. While
playing with it, she got her head stuck into it.
<br> She didn't panic and hit her head into the
stump of the tree to get rid of it.
<br> One day she drenched her head in oil and
the ring moved out of her neck.</p>
</body>
</html>
```

Now I will move on to integrate Polaroid images in the webpages.

```
<html>
<head>
<style>
body {margin: 25px}
```

```
div {

    width: 50%

    background-color: white;

    box-shadow: 0 4px 6px 0 rgba(0, 0, 0, 0.1),
0 4px 15px 0 egba(0, 0, 0, 0.2);

    margin-bottom: 25px;

}
</style>
</head>
<body>
<h1> Let me tell you a story.</h1>
<h2>The story is about an eagle.</h2>
<div>
<img src="eagle.jpg" alt="Eagle"
style="width:50%">
<p> Once, there was an eagle that flew high in
the skies,
<br> touching upon the tip of the mountains.
<br> One day she found a ring, stuck in the
branch of an apple tree.
<br> She took it and flew to her nest. While
playing with it, she got her head stuck in it.
<br> She didn't panic or hit her head on the
stump of a tree to get rid of it.
<br> Instead, she embraced it as a mark of
distinction among fellow eagles.
<br> Then, one day she drenched her head in oil
and the ring came off of her neck.</p>
</body>
```

```
</html>
```

(CSS Styling Images, n.d)

CSS Lists

There are different types of lists known as unordered lists (<ul>) and ordered lists (<ol>). An unordered list is marked with the bullets, and the items of an ordered list are displayed in the form of letters as well as numbers. You can set several list item markers for an ordered list as well as an unordered list. I'll start with the life-style-type property to specify the type of list I am going to use. Let's start creating a code example.

```
<!DOCTYPE html>
<html>
<head>
<style>
ul.1 {
   list-style-type: upper-roman;
}
ul.2 {
   list-style-type: square;
}
ol.3 {
   list-style-type: circle;
}
ol.4 {
   list-style-type: lower-alpha;
```

```
    }
    </style>
    </head>
    <body>
    <p>Let's take a look at at an example of
    unordered lists:</p>
    <ul class="1">
      <li>cucumber</li>
      <li>apple</li>
      <li>guava</li>
    </ul>
    <ul class="2">
      <li>potato</li>
      <li>tomato</li>
      <li>radish</li>
    </ul>
    <p>Let's take a look at at an example of ordered
    lists:</p>
    <ol class="3">
      <li>carrot</li>
      <li>avocado</li>
      <li>strawberry</li>
    </ol>
    <ol class="4">
      <li>blue berry</li>
      <li>grapes</li>
      <li>melon</li>
    </ol>
    </body>
    </html>
```

The result of the code will be as under:

Let's take a look at an example of unordered lists:

- cucumber

- apple

- guava

- potato

- tomato

- radish

Let's take a look at an example of ordered lists:

1. carrot

2. avocado

3. strawberry

1. blueberry

2. grapes

3. melon

We can add colors to CSS lists by the following method. Let's see.

```html
<!DOCTYPE html>
<html>
<head>
<style>
ol {
   background: light blue;
   padding: 20px;
}
ul {
   background: pink;
   padding: 15px;
}
ol li {
   background: gray;
   padding: 25px;
   margin-left: 20px
}
ul li {
   background: gray;
   margin: 5px;
}
</style>
</head>
<body>
<ul>
```

```
<li>potato</li>
<li>tomato</li>
<li>radish</li>
</ul>
<ol>
<li>carrot</li>
<li>avocado</li>
<li>strawberry</li>
</ol>
</body>
</html>
```

The result of the above mentioned code is as under:

Chapter 10

CSS Rounded Corners

To add to the versatility of CSS, there is a border-radius property that gives any HTML element rounded corners. Just imagine what a fine look your web page will give to the visitors if the icons tend to curve at the corners. You can add sophistication to the CSS buttons. The CSS border-radius property defines the radius of a particular HTML element.

In this chapter, I will be explaining the border-radius property in detail so that you may be able to style the buttons and small icons on your website. I will be trying out multiple rounded designs for the buttons so that you will have more than one options for different buttons or different pages of the website. In the next code example, I am going to try out three types of border-radiuses for three different HTML elements. Let's see how to do that.

```
<!DOCTYPE html>
<html>
<head>
<style>
#br1 {
    border-radius: 20px;
    background: #73AD21;
```

```css
  padding: 15px;

  width: 200px;

  height: 100px;

}

#br2 {

  border-radius: 20px;

  border: 2px solid #73AD21;

  padding: 25px;

  width: 150px;

  height: 100px;

}

#br3 {

  border-radius: 20px;

  background: #656565;

  background-position: left top;

  background-repeat: repeat;

  padding: 15px;

  width: 150px;

  height: 100px;

}

#br4 {

  border-radius: 20px;

  background: #35BC51;

  padding: 15px;

  width: 200px;

  height: 170px;
```

```
}
</style>
</head>
<body>
<h1 id="br1">I will tell you a story about an
eagle.</h1>
<p id="br2"> Once, there was an eagle that flew
high in the skies,
<br> touching upon the tip of the mountains.</p>
<p id="br3"> One day she found a ring, stuck in
the branch of an apple tree.</p>
<p id="br4">She took it and flew to her nest.
While playing with it, she got her head stuck in
it.
<br>She didn't panic or hit her head on the
stump of a tree to get rid of it.
<br>One day she drenched her head in oil and the
ring came off of her neck.</p>
</body>
</html>
```

The boxes will appear perfectly round with different shapes and colors. You can take the above code example and try out in code editor to see the result.

Specifying Box Corners

The border-radius property of CSS tends to have around one to four values. There are specific rules to follow for that which we will learn in the practice code. You will have to write them in a consecutive order in which the first value is applied to the top-left corner of the box, the second value represents the top-right corner, and the third value is for the bottom-right corner while the fourth which also is the last is applied to the bottom-left corner of the box. You should remember this order to deliver a perfect result.

If you write three values in the border-radius property, then the first value will represent the top-left corner of the box; the second value will represent the top-right as well as the bottom-left corners while the third value will represent the bottom-right corner of the box. In case the number of values is two, the first values represent top-left as well as bottom-right corners, while the second value is for bottom-left and top-right corners of the box. Last but not least to remember is that if you find out just one value in the border-radius property, it represents all the four corners of the box. In the following code example, I will be trying out all the four types.

```
<!DOCTYPE html>
<html>
<head>
<style>
#br1 {
    border-radius: 15px 40px 30px 5px;
    background: #73AD21;
    padding: 15px;
    width: 200px;
    height: 100px;
}
#br2 {
    border-radius: 15px 50px 30px;
```

```css
    background: #35BC98;

    padding: 25px;

    width: 150px;

    height: 100px;

}

#br3 {

    border-radius: 20px 40px;

    background: #656565;

    padding: 15px;

    width: 150px;

    height: 100px;

}

#br4 {

    border-radius: 20px;

    background: #35BC51;

    padding: 15px;

    width: 200px;

    height: 170px;

}

</style>

</head>

<body>

<h1 id="br1">I will tell you a story about an
eagle.</h1>

<p id="br2"> Once, there was an eagle that flew
high in the skies,

<br> touching upon the tip of the mountains.</p>
```

```
<p id="br3"> One day she found a ring, stuck in
the branch of an apple tree.</p>

<p id="br4">She took it and flew to her nest.
While playing with it, she got her head stuck in
it.

<br>She didn't panic or hit her head on the
stump of a tree to get rid of it.

<br>One day she drenched her head in oil and the
ring came off of her neck.</p>

</body>

</html>
```

If you run this code in the browser, you will see how beautifully the corners of the boxes have been shaped. You can adjust the height and width of the boxes according to the size of the text. I have tested two to three size ranges before I hit upon the right one. Keep changing the values and you will know how to do that in a perfect way.

There is another way to style CSS boxes. You can mold and shape the corners of the boxes in an elliptical form. There will be some changes in the code which you can see in the example given as under:

```
<!DOCTYPE html>

<html>

<head>

<style>

#br1 {
  border-radius: 50px / 20px;
  background: #73AD21;
```

```css
  padding: 15px;

  width: 200px;

  height: 175px;

}

#br2 {

  border-radius: 10px / 40px;

  background: #35BC98;

  padding: 25px;

  width: 150px;

  height: 100px;

}

#br3 {

  border-radius: 60%;

  background: #656565;

  padding: 25px;

  width: 100px;

  height: 100px;

}

#br4 {

  border-radius: 35%;

  background: #35BC51;

  padding: 25px;

  width: 200px;

  height: 170px;

}

</style>
```

```
</head>

<body>

<h1 id="br1">Let me narrate a story of an
eagle.</h1>

<p id="br2"> Once, there was an eagle that flew
high in the skies,

<br> touching upon the tip of the mountains.</p>

<p id="br3"> One day she found a ring, stuck in
the branch of an apple tree.</p>

<p id="br4">She took it and flew to her nest.
While playing with it, she got her head stuck in
it.

<br>She didn't panic or hit her head on the
stump of a tree to get rid of it.

<br>One day she drenched her head in oil and the
ring came off of her neck.</p>

</body>

</html>
```

If you run the above code example in the browser, you will find out
that all the four html elements have different box shapes. In this code
example, I have shown two ways by which you can reshape the
boxes into elliptical form. While the percentage procedure is easier
and more fun to do, the other one, though a bit difficult, is more
thorough and efficient as you have the liberty to delve into minute
details about the shape and adjust slight nuances. Even a plus and
minus of a single number will show its effect on your web design.

CSS Border-Radius Property

This special property allows us to shape corners of CSS borders. I am going to apply the same reshaping style to the borders of html elements. Peruse on the following code example.

```
<!DOCTYPE html>
<html>
<head>
<style>
#br1 {
   border: 2px solid blue;
   border-radius: 50px / 20px;
   padding: 15px;
   width: 200px;
   height: 175px;
}
#br2 {
   border: 2px solid green;
   border-radius: 10px / 40px;
   background: #35BC98;
   padding: 25px;
   width: 150px;
   height: 100px;
}
#br3 {
   border: 2px solid red;
   border-radius: 60%;
```

```css
    background: #656565;

    padding: 25px;

    width: 100px;

    height: 100px;

}

#br4 {

    border-radius: 35%;

    background: #35BC51;

    padding: 25px;

    width: 200px;

    height: 170px;

}

</style>

</head>

<body>

<h1 id="br1">Let me narrate a story of an
eagle.</h1>

<p id="br2"> Once, there was an eagle that flew
high in the skies,

<br> touching upon the tip of the mountains.</p>

<p id="br3"> One day she found a ring, stuck in
the branch of an apple tree.</p>

<p id="br4"> She took it and flew to her nest.
While playing with it, she got her head stuck in
it.

<br>She didn't panic or hit her head on the
stump of a tree to get rid of it.

<br>One day she drenched her head in oil and the
ring came off of her neck</p>
```

```
</body>
</html>
```

Now take the code and try it out in the browser. You should see the corners of the border being reshaped in an elliptical form.

With the CSS border-radius property, you have the freedom to choose which corner you want to specify.

Chapter 11

CSS Layout, Float and Inline-Block

CSS position property allows you to specify the type of positioning method, which you are using to style each HTML element. The position property offers a range of positioning methods for a particular element. These HTML elements include relative, sticky, or static, and fixed. CSS position property allows you to position the HTML element at the top, at the bottom, left and right sides as per your needs. (CSS Layout – The position Property, nd)

You have to set first the position property in the HTML code. This chapter will walk you through a different aspect of a CSS property, which affects the layout of your webpage. Also, it will explain the importance and usage of CSS float property and Inline-block property. Let's see how CSS position property works.

```
<!DOCTYPE html>
<html>
<head>
<style>
h1.static {
    position: static;
    border: 2px solid red;
}
```

```css
div.relative {
    position: relative;
    left: 30px;
    border: 2px green;
}
div.fixed {
    position: fixed;
    bottom: 0;
    right: 0;
    width: 250px;
    border: 2px solid yellow;
}
</style>
</head>
<body>
<h1 class="static">Let me narrate a story of an eagle.</h1>
<div class="relative"> Once, there was an eagle that flew high in the skies,
<br> touching upon the tip of the mountains.</div>
<p> One day she found a ring, stuck in the branch of an apple tree.</p>
<div class="fixed">She took it and flew to her nest. While playing with it, she got her head stuck in it.
<br>She didn't panic or hit her head on the stump of a tree to get rid of it.
```

```
<br>One day she drenched her head in oil and the
ring came off of her neck.</div>
</body>
</html>
```

The code example contains three types of positions for HTML elements. When you run the code in the browser, you will be able to see how it decides the positions of different HTML elements. The static property is the default position of the code. If you have set an HTML element to default, these elements are not going to be affected by the left, right, bottom, and top properties. The relative position of CSS code sets the HTML elements at a position, which is relative to its normal position. For example, you can move an element to the left and right relative to its normal position, which I have demonstrated in the second snippet of code. At the third point comes the fixed position, which positions an HTML element relative to its viewport. It means that it always tends to stay in the same place even if the visitors tend to scroll the page down or up or right or left. This feature comes handy especially when you have to put an important advertisement or announcement on the webpage, which you want your users to stick to. This feature should be used carefully; otherwise, it will turn out to be annoying for the visitors of your website. You should note that a positioned element is the one, which holds any position except static. (CSS Layout – The position Property, nd)

CSS Position: Absolute

This element is positioned relative to the closest ancestor. In case there are no positioned ancestors for the absolute position to stick to, they use the body of the HTML document and move as the user scrolls the page up or down.

```
<!DOCTYPE html>
<html>
<head>
<style>
div.relative {
    position: relative;
    width: 400px;
    height: 200px;
    border: 2px solid green;
}
div.absolute {
    position: absolute;
    top: 70px;
    right: 0;
    width: 250px;
    height: 150px;
    border: 2px solid yellow;
}
</style>
</head>
<body>
<h1>Let me narrate a story of an eagle.</h1>
<div class="relative"> Once, there was an eagle
that flew high in the skies,
```

```
<br> touching upon the tip of the
mountains.</div>

<p> One day she found a ring, stuck in the
branch of an apple tree.</p>

<div class="absolute">She took it and flew to
her nest. While playing with it, she got her
head stuck in it.

<br>She didn't panic or hit her head on the
stump of a tree to get rid of it.

<br>One day she drenched her head in oil and the
ring came off of her neck.</div>

</body>

</html>
```

There is another position named as sticky. It is based on the scroll position of the user. Let's see how to write the code for this position.

```
<!DOCTYPE html>

<html>

<head>

<style>

div.sticky {

    position: -webkit-sticky;

    position: sticky;

    top: 0;

    padding: 10px;

    background-color: #cae8ca;

    border: 2px solid green;

}

</style>
```

```
</head>

<body>

<h1>Let me narrate a story of an eagle.</h1>

<div class="sticky"> Once, there was an eagle
that flew high in the skies,

<br> touching upon the tip of the
mountains.</div>

<p> One day she found a ring, stuck in the
branch of an apple tree.</p>

<p>She took it and flew to her nest. While
playing with it, she got her head stuck in it.

<br>She didn't panic or hit her head on the
stump of a tree to get rid of it.

<br>One day she drenched her head in oil and the
ring came off of her neck.</p>

<p>She took it and flew to her nest. While
playing with it, she got her head stuck in it.

<br>She didn't panic or hit her head on the
stump of a tree to get rid of it.

<br>One day she drenched her head in oil and the
ring came off of her neck.</p>

</body>

</html>
```

I have deliberately copied and pasted the paragraph twice to fill the page with enough text so that you can scroll down and see that the first paragraph sticks at the top of the page and also adjusts to the sides as well. If the text still is not enough, you should zoom in the web page at 200%, and it will work fine and allow you to test the code. (CSS Layout – The position Property, nd)

160

CSS Float and Clear

The CSS float element tends to specify how a certain HTML element can be floated on a web page. This property also specifies what kind of HTML elements can float and on which side. The float property is generally used for positioning as well as formatting the content. Normally, CSS property has four values, such as right, left, none, and inherit. You can use this property to float an image and wrap the text around images.

```
<!DOCTYPE html>
<html>
<head>
<style>
img {
    float: right;
}
</style>
</head>
<body>
<h1>Let me narrate a story of an eagle.</h1>
<p><img src="eagle.jpg" alt="Eagle"
style="width:150px;height:150px;margin-
left:10px;">

Once, there was an eagle that flew high in the
skies,

<br> touching upon the tip of the mountains.

<br> One day she found a ring, stuck in the
branch of an apple tree.</p>
```

```
<p>She took it and flew to her nest. While
playing with it, she got her head stuck in it.
<br>She didn't panic or hit her head on the
stump of a tree to get rid of it.
<br>One day she drenched her head in oil and the
ring came off of her neck.</p>
</body>
</html>
```

You can run the code in the internet browser and see how the image of floats to the right of the corner. I have used the image which I had stored on the computer. You can replace the name of the image in the allotted slot with the one which you want to put on your web page. Note that you should store the image in the same folder where you have stored the HTML page. You can float it to the right of the code just by changing the position. Everything else in the code remains the same. Keep that in mind. See the following example, and don't forget to test the code in the internet browser.

```
<!DOCTYPE html>
<html>
<head>
<style>
img {
    float: left;
}
</style>
</head>
<body>
<h1>Let me narrate a story of an eagle.</h1>
```

```
<p><img src="eagle.jpg" alt="Eagle"
style="width:150px;height:150px;margin-
left:10px;">
```

Once, there was an eagle that flew high in the skies,

```
<br> touching upon the tip of the mountains.
<br> One day she found a ring, stuck in the
branch of an apple tree.</p>
<p>She took it and flew to her nest. While
playing with it, she got her head stuck in it.
<br>She didn't panic or hit her head on the
stump of a tree to get rid of it.
<br>One day she drenched her head in oil and the
ring came off of her neck.</p>
</body>
</html>
```

(CSS Layout - float and clear, n.d)

CSS Layout – Display: Inline-Block

The display: inline-block is special in a way that it allows to fix the height and width of html elements. This particular CSS property respects the CSS margins and paddings, a facility which simple display: inline doesn't offer to programmers. If we compare it with the simple display: block, this particular CSS property cannot add a line-break after an html element. The next code example carries details about three different CSS properties such as display: inline, display: block and display: inline-block.

```
<!DOCTYPE html>
```

```
<html>
<head>
<style>
span.x {
    display: inline;
    width: 150px;
    height: 110px;
    padding: 7px;
    border: 2px solid blue;
    background-color: green;
}
span.y {
    display: inline-block;
    width: 100px;
    height: 50px;
    padding: 7px;
    border: 2px solid blue;
    background-color: yellow;
}
span.z {
    display: block;
    width: 80px;
    height: 80px;
    padding: 7px;
    border: 2px solid blue;
    background-color: light blue;
```

```
}
</style>
</head>
<body>
<h1>Let me narrate a story of an <span
class="x">eagle</span>.</h1>
<p>Once, there was an <span
class="z">eagle</span> which flew high in the
skies,
<br> touching upon the tip of the mountains.
<br> One day she found a <span class="y">
ring</span>, stuck in the branch of an <span
class="z"> apple</span> tree.</p>
<p>She took it and flew to her nest. While
playing with it, she got her head stuck in it.
<br>She didn't panic or hit her head on the
stump of a tree to get rid of it.
<br>One day she drenched her head in oil and the
ring came off of her neck.</p>
</body>
</html>
```

The display in the browser will show the words which I have enclosed in the code brackets, in the color boxes which I have mentioned in the html document. You can change the color, width and height values of the code as per your personalized requirements. (CSS Layout – display: inline-block, n.d)

```
<!DOCTYPE html>
<html>
<head>
```

```
<style>
.navigation {
  background-color: light blue;
  list-style-type: none;
  text-align: left;
  margin: 1px;
  padding: 2px;
}
.navigation li {
  display: inline-block;
  font-size: 15px;
  padding: 20px;
}
</style>
</head>
<body>
<ul class="navigation">
  <li><a href="#The Home Page">The Home
Page</a></li>
  <li><a href="#children's books">Children's
books</a></li>
  <li><a href="#short stories">Short
Stories</a></li>
  <li><a href="#Animated stories">Aniamated
Stories</a></li>
</ul>
<h1>Let me narrate a story of an eagle.</h1>
```

```
<p>Once, there was an eagle that flew high in
the skies,
<br> touching upon the tip of the mountains.
<br> One day she found a ring, stuck in the
branch of an apple tree.</p>
<p>She took it and flew to her nest. While
playing with it, she got her head stuck in it.
<br>She didn't panic or hit her head on the
stump of a tree to get rid of it.
<br>One day she drenched her head in oil and the
ring came off of her neck.</p>
</body>
</html>
```

You can add more links on the website to make it more interactive. Also, change the color, font size and font style of the webpage. (CSS Layout – display: inline-block, n.d)

Pseudo Elements

A CSS pseudo-element in CSS programming language is basically used to style certain parts of an html element. If you master the art of writing pseudo-elements, you can be capable of styling the very first letter of the element and a full line of an html element. There is a slight variation in its use such as the use double colon ::first-line as well as :first-line. This is how programmers were able to distinguish between pseudo-classes as well as pseudo-elements.

The ::first-line pseudo-element is usually used to style the very first line of a piece of text. Let's move on to the html document to style the first line of the html code.

```
<!DOCTYPE html>
<html>
<head>
<style>
p::first-line{
    color: red;
    font-variant: small-caps;
}
</style>
</head>
<body>
<h1>Let me narrate a story of an eagle.</h1>
<p>Once, there was an eagle that flew high in
the skies,
<br> touching upon the tip of the mountains.
<br> One day she found a ring, stuck in the
branch of an apple tree.</p>
</body>
</html>
```

You will see that the first line of code will appear red in the browser.

Chapter 12

Navigation Bar

CSS offers programmers to position certain items in the navigation bar. As a website owner, you want your visitors to navigate through your website and explore your products and services. To achieve this purpose, we have to position the items correctly. We can style them in the horizontal and vertical positions. To do that, we will use the display: inline property, which we already have explored.

Navigation bars are one of the most essential elements to style on a webpage. Thankfully, CSS offers us a wide range of styles to make them look beautiful and attractive. After all, every business owner wants his website to be easy-to-navigate, and colors play a critical role in making it possible. Now, let's us jump to the editor.

A navigation bar is generally a list of HTML elements. You will need the same standard HTML code as a base. It is a collection or a list of links on a webpage that's why we have to use <ul> and <li> elements to create a navigation bar.

```
<!DOCTYPE html>
<html>
<head>
<ul>
```

```
   <li><a href="#home page">The Home
Page</a></li>

   <li><a href="#Kidscorner">Kid's
Corner</a></li>

   <li><a href="#Short Stories">Short
Stories</a></li>

   <li><a href="#Animated">Animated
Videos</a></li>

</ul>

</head>

<body>

<h1>Let me narrate a story of an eagle.</h1>

<p>Once, there was an eagle that flew high in
the skies,

<br> touching upon the tip of the mountains.

<br> One day she found a ring, stuck in the
branch of an apple tree.</p>

</body>

</html>
```

As there are no CSS rules added to the html document, we will have a simple navigation bar which will look like the following:

- The Home Page

- Kid's Corner

- Short Stories

- Animated Videos

Let me narrate a story of an eagle.

Once, there was an eagle that flew high in the skies,
touching upon the tip of the mountains.
One day she found a ring stuck in the branch of an apple tree.

(CSS Navigation Bar, n.d)

It is this list that we have to edit with the help of CSS properties. In the next code example, I will explain how we can turn that simple HTML list into a navigation bar. I will be removing bullets from the list mentioned above along with its default margin and padding.

```
<!DOCTYPE html>
<html>
<head>
<style>
ul {
    list-style-type: none;
    padding: 0;
    margin: 0;
}
</style>
</head>
<body>
<ul>
  <li><a href="#home page">The Home
Page</a></li>
```

```
<li><a href="#Kidscorner">Kid's
Corner</a></li>

<li><a href="#Short Stories">Short
Stories</a></li>

<li><a href="#Animated">Animated
Videos</a></li>

</ul>

<h1>Let me narrate a story of an eagle.</h1>

<p>Once, there was an eagle that flew high in
the skies,

<br> touching upon the tip of the mountains.

<br> One day she found a ring, stuck in the
branch of an apple tree.</p>

<p>She took it and flew to her nest. While
playing with it, she got her head stuck in it.

<br>She didn't panic or hit her head on the
stump of a tree to get rid of it.

<br>One day she drenched her head in oil and the
ring came off of her neck.</p>

</body>

</html>
```

In the result of the code, you can see that the list no longer looks like a list. CSS has successfully transformed it into a navigation bar.

The Home Page

Kid's Corner

Short Stories

Animated Videos

Let me narrate a story of an eagle.

Once, there was an eagle that flew high in the skies,
touching upon the tip of the mountains.
One day she found a ring stuck in the branch of an apple tree.

She took it and flew to her nest. While playing with it, she got her
head stuck in it.
She didn't panic or hit her head on the stump of the tree to get rid of
it.
One day she drenched her head in oil, and the ring came off of her
neck.

(CSS Navigation Bar, n.d)

Vertical Navigation Bar

You can build a vertical navigation bar by integrating the <a>
element inside an html list. The rest of the code will remain the
same. Let's move to create a vertical navigation bar for your
webpage.

```
<!DOCTYPE html>
<html>
<head>
<style>
ul {
    list-style-type: none;
    padding: 0;
```

```
        margin: 0;
}
li a {
        display: block;
        width: 80px;
        background-color: light blue;
}
</style>
</head>
<body>
<ul>
    <li><a href="#home page">The Home
Page</a></li>
    <li><a href="#Kidscorner">Kid's
Corner</a></li>
    <li><a href="#Short Stories">Short
Stories</a></li>
    <li><a href="#Animated">Animated
Videos</a></li>
</ul>
<h1>Let me narrate a story of an eagle.</h1>
<p>Once, there was an eagle that flew high in
the skies,
<br> touching upon the tip of the mountains.
<br> One day she found a ring, stuck in the
branch of an apple tree.</p>
<p>She took it and flew to her nest. While
playing with it, she got her head stuck in it.
```

```
<br>She didn't panic or hit her head on the
stump of a tree to get rid of it.

<br>One day she drenched her head in oil and the
ring came off of her neck.</p>

</body>

</html>
```

(CSS Navigation Bar, n.d)

CSS navigation bar is amazing due to the fact that you get to work on a diverse range of styles. You can create a simple vertical navigation bar which has a light blue background. The background color of the links will change when you tend to move your mouse over the bar. This interactive navigation bar is amazing in engaging visitors of your website.

```
<!DOCTYPE html>

<html>

<head>

<style>

ul {

    list-style-type: none;

    padding: 0;

    margin: 0;

    width: 300px;

    background-color: #f2f2f2;

}

li a {

    display: block;
```

```
      width: 150px;

      color: #555;

      text-decoration: none;

}

li a:hover {

      background-color: pink;

      color:white;

}

</style>

</head>

<body>

<ul>

   <li><a href="#home page">The Home
Page</a></li>

   <li><a href="#Kidscorner">Kid's
Corner</a></li>

   <li><a href="#Short Stories">Short
Stories</a></li>

   <li><a href="#Animated">Animated
Videos</a></li>

</ul>

<h1> Let me narrate a story of an eagle.</h1>

<p> Once, there was an eagle that flew high in
the skies,

<br> touching upon the tip of the mountains.

<br> One day she found a ring, stuck in the
branch of an apple tree.</p>

</body>
```

```
</html>
```

(CSS Navigation Bar, n.d)

If you run the code example in the browser, you will see that when you hover the mouse pointer over the navigation bar, its color will turn to pink. Upon moving the mouse pointer away, the color will get back to normal. That's you can make your page highly interactive and user-friendly.

Also, you can add an active class to the links inside the html code, which tells the user about the page he or she is on.

```
<!DOCTYPE html>
<html>
<head>
<style>
ul {
    list-style-type: none;
    padding: 0;
    margin: 0;
    width: 300px;
    background-color: #f2f2f2;
}
li a {
    display: block;
    padding: 6px 12px;
    color: #555;
    text-decoration: none;
```

```
}
li a.active {
    background-color: light blue;
    color: white;
}
li a:hover {
    background-color: pink;
    color:white;
}
</style>
</head>
<body>
<ul>
  <li><a href="The Home Page">Home</a></li>
  <li><a class="active" href="#Kidscorner">Kid's
Corner</a></li>
  <li><a href="#Short Stories">Short
Stories</a></li>
  <li><a href="#Animated">Animated
Videos</a></li>
</ul>
<h1> Let me narrate a story of an eagle.</h1>
<p> Once, there was an eagle that flew high in
the skies,
<br> touching upon the tip of the mountains.
<br> One day she found a ring, stuck in the
branch of an apple tree.</p>
</body>
```

```
</html>
```

(CSS Navigation Bar, n.d)

The link of the page the visitor is on will be displayed in light blue color as you will see if you run the code in the internet browser. The rest of the links will be displayed as pink when you hover the mouse over them.

CSS navigation bar property gives you the freedom to adjust the alignment of the text inside the links. You can put them in the center and also add borders to make them look better to the eyes of the visitors of your website.

```
<!DOCTYPE html>
<html>
<head>
<style>
ul {
    list-style-type: none;
    padding: 0;
    margin: 0;
    width: 300px;
    background-color: #f2f2f2;
    border: 2px solid navy;
}
li a {
    display: block;
    padding: 6px 12px;
```

```
        color: #000;
        text-decoration: none;
}
li {
        text-align: center;
        border-bottom: 2px solid navy;
}
li a.active {
        background-color: light blue;
        color: white;
}
li a:hover:not(.active) {
        background-color: pink;
        color:white;
}
</style>
</head>
<body>
<ul>
   <li><a href="The Home Page">Home</a></li>
   <li><a class="active" href="#Kidscorner">Kid's
Corner</a></li>
   <li><a href="#Short Stories">Short
Stories</a></li>
   <li><a href="#Animated">Animated
Videos</a></li>
</ul>
```

```
<h1> Let me narrate a story of an eagle.</h1>
<p> Once, there was an eagle that flew high in
the skies,
<br> touching upon the tip of the mountains.
<br> One day she found a ring, stuck in the
branch of an apple tree.</p>
</body>
</html>
```

You will be able to see a display in which all the links on your webpage will appear centralized. I have also added the border property and its color is navy blue. You can see how transformed the list of links look on the webpage. Like every other web page, you can adjust the height and width of the website.

If you are a regular surfer of the internet, you might have come across a few websites which offer a vertical navigation bar to the right or left side of the website, which tends to stick on the screen even if you are scrolling down or up. CSS navigation bar property allows you to create a similar thing on your website. It will add more beauty and glamor to your webpage. Visitors highly appreciate this kind of sophistication as they deem it more reliable. (CSS Navigation Bar, n.d)

```
<!DOCTYPE html>
<html>
<head>
<style>
body {
    margin: 0;
```

```css
}
ul {
    list-style-type: none;
    padding: 0;
    margin: 0;
    width: 300px;
    background-color: #f2f2f2;
    position: fixed;
    height: 110%
    overflow: auto;
}
li a {
    display: block;
    padding: 6px 12px;
    color: #000;
    text-decoration: none;
}
li a.active {
    background-color: light blue;
    color: white;
}
li a:hover:not(.active) {
    background-color: pink;
    color:white;
}
</style>
```

```html
</head>
<body>
<ul>
  <li><a href="The Home Page">Home</a></li>
  <li><a class="active" href="#Kidscorner">Kid's
Corner</a></li>
  <li><a href="#Short Stories">Short
Stories</a></li>
  <li><a href="#Animated">Animated
Videos</a></li>
</ul>
<div style="margin-left:25%;padding:2px
10px:height:1000px;">
<h1> Let me narrate a story of an eagle.</h1>
<p> Once, there was an eagle that flew high in
the skies,
<br> touching upon the tip of the mountains.
<br> One day she found a ring, stuck in the
branch of an apple tree.</p>
<br>She took it and flew to her nest. While
playing with it, she got her head stuck in it.
<br>She didn't panic or hit her head on the
stump of a tree to get rid of it.
<br>One day she drenched her head in oil and the
ring came off of her neck.</p>
<p> Once, there was an eagle that flew high in
the skies,
<br> touching upon the tip of the mountains.
<br> One day she found a ring, stuck in the
branch of an apple tree.</p>
```

```
<br>She took it and flew to her nest. While
playing with it, she got her head stuck in it.

<br>She didn't panic or hit her head on the
stump of a tree to get rid of it.

<br>One day she drenched her head in oil and the
ring came off of her neck.</p>

</div>

</body>

</html>
```

(CSS Navigation Bar, n.d)

In the browser, you will be able to see the navigation bar stuck on the right side. I have doubled up the amount of text so that the page appears full. You can zoom it if it doesn't extend over to the second page. Now scroll down and up. The navigation bar should stick to the side of the web page. You can change the colors of links, the background and the size of the navigation bar to suit your requirements.

Horizontal Navigation Bar

Up till now, we had been talking about different styles of vertical navigation bars. Now we should move on to the horizontal navigate bars, which are the most common among web designers. Like the vertical navigation bar, horizontal navigation is also easy to make and style. Let's create a horizontal navigation bar, which has a navy blue background and which changes the color of the links when visitors hover the mouse over them. Sounds similar to what you have already learned? There is a slight difference in the code. Let's write it in the editor.

```
<!DOCTYPE html>
<html>
<head>
<style>
ul {
    list-style-type: none;
    padding: 0;
    margin: 0;
    overflow: hidden;
    background-color: #555;
}
li {
    float: left;
}
li a {
    display: block;
    padding: 6px 12px;
    color: white;
    text-align: center;
    text-decoration: none;
}
li a:hover {
    background-color: green;
}
</style>
</head>
```

```
<body>
<ul>
  <li><a href="The Home Page">Home</a></li>
  <li><a href="#Kidscorner">Kid's
Corner</a></li>
  <li><a href="#Short Stories">Short
Stories</a></li>
  <li><a href="#Animated">Animated
Videos</a></li>
</ul>
<div style="margin-left:25%;padding:2px
10px:height:1000px;">
<h1><b> Let me narrate a story of an
eagle.</b></h1>
<p> Once, there was an eagle that flew high in
the skies,
<br> touching upon the tip of the mountains.
<br> One day she found a ring, stuck in the
branch of an apple tree.</p>
</p>
</div>
</body>
</html>
```

Just as we did with the vertical navigation bars, we will add an active class to the horizontal navigation bar to tell the user on which page he is. In the following code example, I have added the active value to add the class property. Now the visitors of your website will see navy blue color on the link which they are visiting at the current moment.

186

```
<!DOCTYPE html>
<html>
<head>
<style>
ul {
    list-style-type: none;
    padding: 0;
    margin: 0;
    overflow: hidden;
    background-color: #999999;
}
li {
    float: left;
}
li a {
    display: block;
    padding: 6px 12px;
    color: white;
    text-align: center;
    text-decoration: none;
}
li a:hover {
    background-color: green;
}
.active {
    background-color: navy;
```

```
}
</style>
</head>
<body>
<ul>
  <li><a href="The Home Page">Home</a></li>
  <li><a class="active" href="#Kidscorner">Kid's
Corner</a></li>
  <li><a href="#Short Stories">Short
Stories</a></li>
  <li><a href="#Animated">Animated
Videos</a></li>
</ul>
<div style="margin-left:25%;padding:2px
10px:height:1000px;">
<h1><b> Let me narrate a story of an
eagle.</b></h1>
<p> Once, there was an eagle that flew high in
the skies,
<br> touching upon the tip of the mountains.
<br> One day she found a ring, stuck in the
branch of an apple tree.</p>
</p>
</div>
</body>
</html>
```

(CSS Navigation Bar, n.d)

Now, we should go on and add the float property to our horizontal navigation bar, which will float one of the list items to the right side. Did it tickle you? Let's do that in the code editor.

```
<!DOCTYPE html>
<html>
<head>
<style>
ul {
    list-style-type: none;
    padding: 0;
    margin: 0;
    overflow: hidden;
    background-color: #999999;
}
li {
    float: left;
}
li a {
    display: block;
    padding: 6px 12px;
    color: white;
    text-align: center;
    text-decoration: none;
}
li a:hover {
    background-color: green;
```

```
}
.active {
    background-color: navy;
}
</style>
</head>
<body>
<ul>
  <li><a href="The Home Page">Home</a></li>
  <li style="float:right"> <a class="active"
href="#Kidscorner">Kid's Corner</a></li>
  <li><a href="#Short Stories">Short
Stories</a></li>
  <li><a href="#Animated">Animated
Videos</a></li>
</ul>
<div style="margin-left:25%;padding:2px
10px:height:1000px;">
<h1><b> Let me narrate a story of an
eagle.</b></h1>
<p> Once, there was an eagle that flew high in
the skies,
<br> touching upon the tip of the mountains.
<br> One day she found a ring, stuck in the
branch of an apple tree.</p>
</p>
</div>
</body>
</html>
```

Please run the code example in the browser. Does it look perfect? Is anything missing in the display? Do you think the way links are being represented on the webpage is perfect or can you improve it so that your users will have a better experience? The links don't appear neat on the webpage, to say the least. What if we divide them by borders? Let's try it out.

```
<!DOCTYPE html>
<html>
<head>
<style>
ul {
    list-style-type: none;
    padding: 0;
    margin: 0;
    overflow: hidden;
    background-color: #999999;
}
li {
    float: left;
    border-right: 2px solid #bbb;
}
li a {
    display: block;
    padding: 6px 12px;
    color: white;
    text-align: center;
    text-decoration: none;
```

```
}
li:last-child {
    border-right: none;
}
li a:hover {
    background-color: green;
}
.active {
    background-color: navy;
}
</style>
</head>
<body>
<ul>
  <li><a class="active" href="The Home
Page">Home</a></li>
  <li style="float:right"> <a class="active"
href="#Kidscorner">Kid's Corner</a></li>
  <li><a href="#Short Stories">Short
Stories</a></li>
  <li><a href="#Animated">Animated
Videos</a></li>
</ul>
<div style="margin-left:25%;padding:2px
10px:height:1000px;">
<h1><b> Let me narrate a story of an
eagle.</b></h1>
<p> Once, there was an eagle that flew high in
the skies,
```

```
<br> touching upon the tip of the mountains.
<br> One day she found a ring, stuck in the
branch of an apple tree.</p>
</p>
</div>
</body>
</html>
```

(CSS Navigation Bar, n.d)

The Fixed Navigation Bar

As we have seen in the vertical navigation bars, you also can fix the horizontal navigation bar. When you will scroll up or down, the page will move but the navigation will stay at the top of the page. The code example for fixing the navigation bar is as under:

```
<!DOCTYPE html>
<html>
<head>
<style>
body {margin:0;}
ul {
    list-style-type: none;
    padding: 0;
    margin: 0;
    overflow: hidden;
    background-color: #999999;
    position: fixed;
```

```
        width: 120%;
        top: 0;
}
li {
        float: left;
        border-right: 2px solid #bbb;
}
li a {
        display: block;
        padding: 6px 12px;
        color: white;
        text-align: center;
        text-decoration: none;
}
li a:hover:not(.active) {
        background-color: green;
}
.active {
        background-color: navy;
}
</style>
</head>
<body>
<ul>
   <li><a class="active" href="The Home
Page">Home</a></li>
```

```html
   <li><a href="#Kidscorner">Kid's
Corner</a></li>

   <li><a href="#Short Stories">Short
Stories</a></li>

   <li><a href="#Animated">Animated
Videos</a></li>

</ul>

<div style="padding:20px;margin-
top:32px;background-color:pink;height:1700px">

<h1><b> Let me narrate a story of an
eagle.</b></h1>

<p> Once, there was an eagle that flew high in
the skies,

<br> touching upon the tip of the mountains.

<br> One day she found a ring, stuck in the
branch of an apple tree.</p>

<br>She took it and flew to her nest. While
playing with it, she got her head stuck in it.

<br>She didn't panic or hit her head on the
stump of a tree to get rid of it.

<br>One day she drenched her head in oil and the
ring came off of her neck.</p>

<br> She took it and flew to her nest. While
playing with it, she got her head stuck into it.

<br> She didn't panic and hit her head into the
stump of the tree to get rid of it.

<br> One day she drenched her head in oil and
the ring moved out of her neck.</p>

<br> She took it and flew to her nest. While
playing with it, she got her head stuck in it.
```

```
<br>She didn't panic or hit her head on the
stump of a tree to get rid of it.
<br>One day she drenched her head in oil and the
ring came off of her neck.</p>
</p>
</div>
</body>
</html>
```

(CSS Navigation Bar, n.d)

Once again, while running the code, keep in mind that you have to zoom in if the text is not enough to fill in the entire page and extend down. Zoom in at 200% and you will be able to test the code. Now scroll down and up, and see the navigation bar will stay tucked at the top. This feature allows the user to jump to another page without getting to the top by scrolling.

So, this feature adds to the ease which you always want to provide to your visitors. What else is easier and beneficial for the visitors than cutting down on the scroll time? So, give it a try on your website and make things happen. You are likely to see substantial growth in the number of visitors on your website. This is simple. Do you like to visit a website that wastes your time? Everyone has to wrap up lots of business matters within a concise period. By adding features that save their time, you can improve on the user experience up to a great extent. Let's take the navigation bar to the bottom of the webpage. The code example is as under:

```
<!DOCTYPE html>
<html>
```

```
<head>
<style>
body {margin:0;}
ul {
    list-style-type: none;
    padding: 0;
    margin: 0;
    overflow: hidden;
    background-color: #999999;
    position: fixed;
    width: 120%;
    bottom: 0;
}
li {
    float: left;
    border-right: 2px solid #bbb;
}
li a {
    display: block;
    padding: 6px 12px;
    color: white;
    text-align: center;
    text-decoration: none;
}
li a:hover:not(.active) {
    background-color: green;
```

```
}
.active {
    background-color: navy;
}
</style>
</head>
<body>
<ul>
  <li><a class="active" href="The Home
Page">Home</a></li>
  <li><a href="#Kidscorner">Kid's
Corner</a></li>
  <li><a href="#Short Stories">Short
Stories</a></li>
  <li><a href="#Animated">Animated
Videos</a></li>
</ul>
<div style="padding:20px;margin-
top:32px;background-color:pink;height:1700px">
<h1><b> Let me narrate a story of an
eagle.</b></h1>
<p> Once, there was an eagle that flew high in
the skies,
<br> touching upon the tip of the mountains.
<br> One day she found a ring, stuck in the
branch of an apple tree.</p>
</p>
</div>
</body>
```

```
</html>
```

Sticky Navigation Bar

I hope you have already digested the CSS styles which I have
explained up till now. Time to jump to the sticky navbar which is
more interactive than the fixed navbar. A sticky navigation bar tends
to shuttle between relative as well as fixed positions when a user
scrolls up and down the webpage. The navigation bar tends to be
positioned in a relative position until it reaches an offset position in
the viewport. After that it tends to stick in place.

```
<!DOCTYPE html>
<html>
<head>
<style>
body {font-size:22px;}
ul {
    list-style-type: none;
    padding: 0;
    margin: 0;
    overflow: hidden;
    background-color: #999999;
    position: -webkit-sticky;
    position: sticky;
    top: 0;
}
li {
    float: left;
```

```
}
li a {
    display: block;
    padding: 6px 12px;
    color: white;
    text-align: center;
    text-decoration: none;
}
li a:hover {
    background-color: green;
}
.active {
    background-color: navy;
}
</style>
</head>
<body>
<div class="header">
<h1><b> Let me narrate a story of an
eagle.</b></h1>
</div>
<ul>
  <li><a class="active" href="The Home
Page">Home</a></li>
  <li><a href="#Kidscorner">Kid's
Corner</a></li>
  <li><a href="#Short Stories">Short
Stories</a></li>
```

```html
    <li><a href="#Animated">Animated
Videos</a></li>

</ul>

<p> Once, there was an eagle that flew high in
the skies,

<br> touching upon the tip of the mountains.

<br> One day she found a ring, stuck in the
branch of an apple tree.</p>

<br>She took it and flew to her nest. While
playing with it, she got her head stuck in it.

<br>She didn't panic or hit her head on the
stump of a tree to get rid of it.

<br>One day she drenched her head in oil and the
ring came off of her neck.</p>

<br>She took it and flew to her nest. While
playing with it, she got her head stuck in it.

<br>She didn't panic or hit her head on the
stump of a tree to get rid of it.

<br>One day she drenched her head in oil and the
ring came off of her neck.</p>

</p>

</div>

</body>

</html>
```

(CSS Navigation Bar, n.d)

Conclusion

CSS is the most viable way to have control over how your web page looks. It allows you to have control over the fonts, colors, margins, text, backgrounds, colors, tables, forms, images, and lists. Now that you have reached the end of the book, you have gone through some uses of the CSS language. You have also realized by now how vital CSS is for your website.

In today's fast age, you can take a free web template from anywhere and build a website in no time. But the question is that will it appeal to the visitors to your website? Will it stand out among hundreds of thousands website? No. You have to customize your website to make things happen.

You can also hire a web designer to build a website for your business, but it just sounds easy. In reality, it is one of the most expensive and exhaustive things to opt for. Web designers don't work for free. You have to pay them loads of cash for designing your website. The same money can be invested in your business, and you can earn plenty of profit from it. So, learning CSS will help you save lots of money and time. Now that you have learned the basics of CSS, you will be able to understand your website design better. You can modify it from time to time, and also, you can renovate the design as per your requirements.

Even if you are not a business owner or you don't have a personal website to design, you can apply the knowledge that you have gained on designing websites for other people. You can make lots of money by starting your own freelance business as a web designer. You can take up contracts for redesigning of old websites. This is far easier and less time-consuming. You can change the color schemes, add new images, forms, and lists. Also, you can remove the old buttons and add new ones as per your personalized requirements. You know what? You can do that within a few hours.

In this book, you have learned all the tricks and tips to kick off your web designing venture. You have learned about CSS background, borders, lists, forms, images, and padding. There were lots of other topics in the lessons that I have tried to cover. You have learned how you can create CSS rules and how you can apply them on HTML elements.

CSS offers you an opportunity to create a wide range of websites that tend to look different from one another. It is the diversity of CSS applications that makes it a top-notch language. The best thing is that unlike other computer languages, you don't need lots of coding to make things happen. Also, the coding is so easy that you start learning and applying it on your first read. The code is easier to read and understand even if written by some other web designer. You can use different CSS rules on a similar HTML element. The content of the HTML element will not be affected at all during the process of styling the page. CSS remains one of the most desired languages because of the diversity of applications it has to offer.

References

CSS Syntax. (n.d). Retrieved from
https://www.w3schools.com/css/css_syntax.asp

CSS Selectors. (n.d). Retrieved from
https://www.w3schools.com/css/css_selectors.asp

CSS Fonts. (n.d). Retrieved from
https://www.w3schools.com/css/css_font.asp

CSS Colors. (n.d). Retrieved from
file:///C:/Users/saifia%20computers/Desktop/css/new%201.html

CSS Tables. (n.d). Retrieved from
https://www.w3schools.com/css/css_table.asp

CSS Borders. (n.d). Retrieved from
https://www.w3schools.com/css/css_border.asp

CSS Outline. (n.d). Retrieved from
https://www.w3schools.com/css/css_outline.asp

CSS Links. (n.d). Retrieved from
https://www.w3schools.com/css/css_link.asp

CSS Forms. (n.d). Retrieved from
https://www.w3schools.com/css/css_form.asp

CSS Layout – display: inline-block. (n.d). Retrieved from
https://www.w3schools.com/css/css_inline-block.asp

CSS Layout – float and clear. (n.d). Retrieved from
https://www.w3schools.com/css/css_float.asp

CSS Margins. (n.d). Retrieved from
https://www.w3schools.com/css/css_margin.asp

CSS Padding. (n.d). Retrieved from
https://www.w3schools.com/css/css_padding.asp

CSS Styling Images. (n.d). Retreived from
https://www.w3schools.com/css/css3_images.asp

CSS Styling Images.. (n.d). Retrieved from
https://www.w3schools.com/css/css3_images.asp

CSS Layout – The position Property. (n.d). Retrieved from
https://www.w3schools.com/css/css_positioning.asp

CSS Navigation Bar. (n.d). Retrieved from
https://www.w3schools.com/css/css_navbar.asp

Duckett, J. (2011). HTML&CSS design and build websites [pdf].
Retrieved from https://wtf.tw/ref/duckett.pdf

How To Add CSS. (n.d). Retrieved from
https://www.w3schools.com/css/css_howto.asp